Chichester Harbour
A Walker's Guide

Chichester Harbour is an Area of Outstanding Natural Beauty on the south coast of Britain. Virtually flat with far reaching sea views, the Harbour is a pleasure for walkers of all abilities. This second edition of *A Walker's Guide* features updated directions, an additional cycle route and new photographs.

Happy Walking

Published by
Chichester Harbour Conservancy,
Harbour Office, Itchenor,
Chichester, PO20 7AW

Chichester
Harbour
Conservancy

www.conservancy.co.uk

Design and Layout by Pafford Design Limited www.pafford-design.co.uk
Printed in Great Britain by Senator Press

ISBN 978 0 9548135 2 9

Chichester Harbour Area of Outstanding Natural Beauty

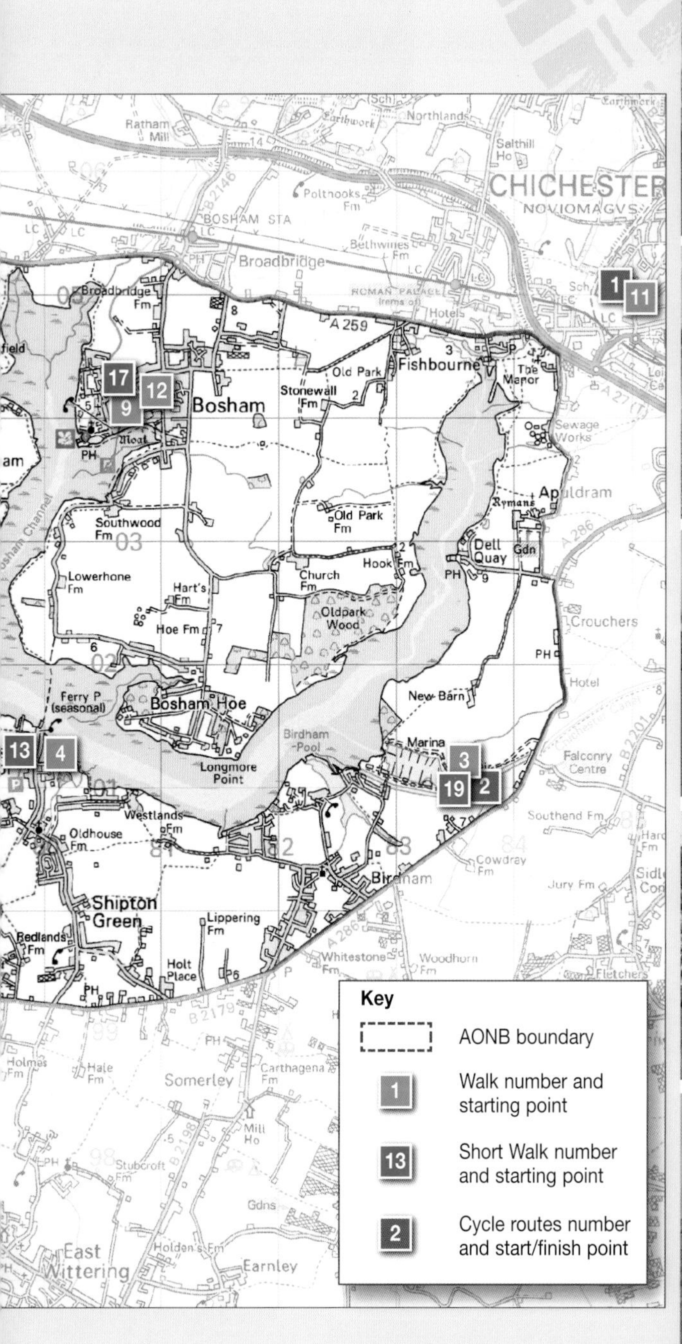
Ratham Mill
Northlands
Salthill Ho
CHICHESTER
NOVIOMAGVS
Poltnooks Fm
BOSHAM STA
Broadbridge
Bethwines Fm
ROMAN PALACE
Hotels
Broadbridge Fm
A 259
Fishbourne
The Manor
Old Park
Stonewall Fm
Bosham
Moat
Sewage Works
Apuldram
Rymans
Southwood Fm
Old Park Fm
Dell Quay
Gdn
Lowerhone Fm
Church Fm
Hook Fm
Hart's Fm
Hoe Fm
Oldpark Wood
Crouchers
Hotel
Ferry P (seasonal)
Bosham Hoe
New Barn
Birdham Pool
Marina
Longmore Point
Falconry Centre
Westlands Fm
Oldhouse Fm
Southend Fm
Cowdray Fm
Birdham
Jury Fm
Shipton Green
Lippering Fm
Redlands Fm
Holt Place
Whitestone Fm
Woodhorn Fm
Fletchers
Holmes Fm
Hale Fm
Somerley
Carthagena Fm
Mill Ho
Stubcroft Fm
Gdns
East Wittering
Holden's Fm
Earnley
Key
AONB boundary
1 Walk number and starting point
13 Short Walk number and starting point
2 Cycle routes number and start/finish point

Long Walks

Short Strolls and Wheelchair Walks

Cycle Routes

Useful Information

Directions
All the walks were tested in 2013. Please note, however, that some footpaths may be diverted and buildings such as pubs may have changed their name since the walks were written. If you have any comments please send them to the Harbour Office to be considered for the next edition.

Distances and Timings
All distances and timings are approximate.

Maps
The maps provided are a guide and are not to scale. Please use OS Explorer Map 120 (Chichester).

Map References
The reference given is for the start point of the walk.

Public Transport
Buses: Stagecoach run most of the local buses. Timetable details are at **www.stagecoachbus.com/south** or telephone **0871 200 22 33** (10p per minute).
For the Selsey – Itchenor service see **www.compass-travel.co.uk**
Trains: Timetable information is at **www.nationalrail.co.uk** or telephone **08457 48 49 50**.

Stiles and Gates
Please note stiles are gradually being replaced with gates where appropriate. This may affect some of the walk directions and photos.

Tides
Please note some paths are flooded at high tide. If you have misjudged the times, you usually only have to wait a short while before the path is clear enough to use. Tide times can be found at **www.conservancy.co.uk** or from the Harbour Office; please note these are only a prediction and factors such as low pressure can make the tide higher than expected.

Tourist Information
Chichester: www.visitchichester.org or telephone **01243 775888.**
Hayling Island: www.visithavant.co.uk or telephone **023 9246 7111**.

Weather
Please check the weather before starting your walk and take the appropriate clothing.
Weather forecasts can be found at **www.conservancy.co.uk** or from the local tourist offices.

Acknowledgements
All walks were written and photographed by Ali Beckett for Chichester Harbour Conservancy.
Design work on the book was undertaken by Neil Pafford at Pafford Design.
Funding was generously provided by the Friends of Chichester Harbour.

The Countryside Code

Respect. Protect. Enjoy

Respect other people

- Consider the local community and other people enjoying the outdoors
- Leave gates and property as you find them and follow paths unless wider access is available

Protect the natural environment

- Leave no trace of your visit and take your litter home
- Keep dogs under effective control

Enjoy the outdoors

- Plan ahead and be prepared
- Follow advice and local signs

1 | **8km/5 miles** | **2.5 hours** | **Map Ref. SU 749 055** - Ordnance Survey Explorer 120

Walk 1

Emsworth to Langstone

This is an 8km walk between Emsworth and Langstone. It uses shoreline paths and an inland route passing Warblington church and an attractive area of woodland. There are plenty of benches on this route, so take time to stop and admire the view and maybe have a chat with the friendly locals who regularly use this path.

Start Point
The Quay, Emsworth PO10 7EQ or The Ship Langstone PO9 1RD
(The walk directions take you from Emsworth to Langstone but it is fully described in both directions so you can start the walk just as easily from Langstone).

By Road
Emsworth - There is a pay and display car park in South Street, Emsworth. From there turn right and you will shortly reach the Quay.
Langstone - There is a free car park at The Ship which is on the left just before the bridge onto Hayling Island.

By Bus
Emsworth - From the east, the Coastliner Service 700 stops at Emsworth Square. From there walk down South Street to the Quay. From the west, the bus stops on the A259. Cross the road using the underpass and walk down North Street to the Square and then down to the Quay.
Langstone - Service 30/31 from Havant to Hayling Island stops at The Ship.

Refreshments
The Ship and The Royal Oak, Langstone and numerous restaurants, pubs and cafés at Emsworth.

Toilets
In the car park, South Street Emsworth and also in the car park at Langstone.

Tides
Tide times must be consulted as part of the shoreline floods between points 3 and 5 when the tide is higher than 4.2m. Avoid walking at least one hour either side of the high tide.

Walk Directions
From the Quay take the path onto the seawall (1) continuing right round until you pass Emsworth Sailing Club.

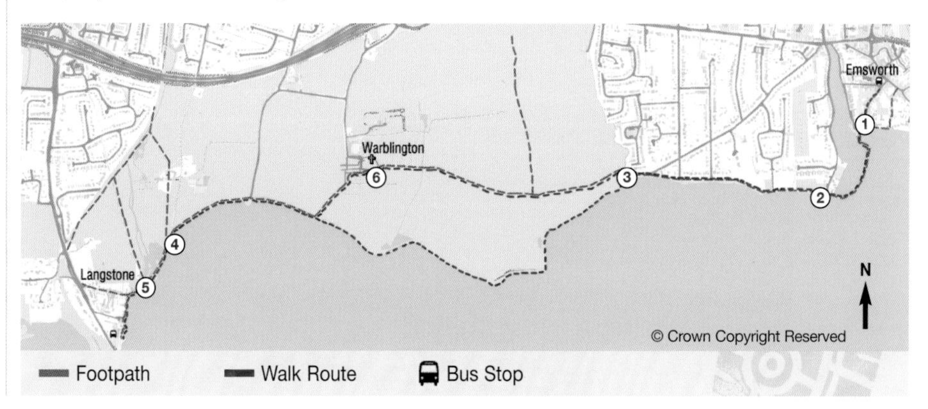

3

Take the small path alongside the flint wall (2), follow it onto the concrete shoreline path. From here you have panoramic views down the Emsworth Channel and towards Northney and Portsmouth.

The path narrows as you near an area of woodland, Nore Barn Woods, and drops down onto the shingle. Ahead the path forks, take the shoreline path, keeping the woodland on your right (3).

4

At the end of the woodland, you will rejoin the shoreline. Shortly you will be able to see Langstone in the distance. Look out for the Spinnaker Tower, Portsmouth.

You will come to an area with upright railway sleepers used as sea defences. At the end of this section, go up the concrete ramp (4) and then follow the path along the seawall to the Mill Pond.

Keep going along this path, you will pass The Royal Oak and cross the High Street (5) then along the raised path by the flint wall before shortly reaching The Ship. When you are ready to return, retrace your steps to the second set of wooden steps.

If you are starting at Langstone, cross the car park and take the path at the far end with a brick wall on your left. Continue along this route, crossing the High Street and passing The Royal Oak. The path continues behind the old mill, now a private house, and past the Mill Pond. After a short way it drops down a concrete ramp to the shoreline then shortly up another concrete ramp to the footpath.

Go through the metal kissing gate to take the path diagonally across a field to the cemetery.

Follow the footpath signs through the cemetery to the exit. From here take the path along the side of the churchyard wall (6).

Keep going straight on through a number of gates and along fields until you come to the corner of a woodland, Nore Barn Woods.

Take the path straight ahead keeping the woodland on your right.

At the end of the woodland, continue straight ahead taking the path along the seawall. You will come onto Western Parade with some housing on your left and then pass a dinghy park before reaching Emsworth Sailing Club.

Follow the footpath onto the Mill Pond wall and continue right round until you reach the Quay.

You are now at the bottom of South Street and can return to your car or the bus stop or if you are returning to Langstone follow the directions from the start.

Extra Items of Interest

Warblington Church
The church is 13th century with Saxon origins. In the churchyard are two unusual 'gravewatchers' huts'. Ahead you can see the remains of Warblington Castle (it is privately owned and not open to the public). The castle was built in the 16th century for Margaret, Countess of Salisbury; later when the manor passed to the Cotton family, Queen Elizabeth was entertained there. In the Civil War it was taken and destroyed by the Parliamentarians, leaving only one tower remaining.

Emsworth Sailing Clubs
There are two sailing clubs and a cruising association in the town. The Slipper Sailing Club is on the Quay at Emsworth. This club was formally founded in 1921 as the Emsworth Mud Slippers Sailing Club. In 1963 they purchased The Anchor in South Street which has since been transformed into a fine clubhouse.

Emsworth Sailing Club is at the other end of the Mill Pond wall in Bath Road. The club was inaugurated in 1919 in the former bathing house. The club prides itself on a huge and distinguished membership which has included Lord Louis Mountbatten who was Commodore in 1931. In addition Sir Peter Blake was a member before he was tragically murdered by pirates in the Amazon in 2001. Sir Peter's grave is in Warblington cemetery.

The Wadeway
On the shoreline at the end of the High Street, Langstone are the remains of a hardened causeway which originally crossed the channel linking the mainland to Hayling Island at low tide. Written references to the Wadeway date back to 1552 and refer to a toll for crossing the causeway. However, carbon dating dates it to early Medieval times. The decline of the Wadeway began in 1817 when permission was granted for the construction of a bridge. In 1821 the causeway was severed by 'New Cut' which was part of the construction of the Portsmouth to Arundel canal making the Wadeway unusable.

2 | **6.5km/4 miles** | **2 hours** | **Map Ref. SU 788 054** - Ordnance Survey Explorer 120

Walk 2
Nutbourne Circular

This 6.5km walk starts at a community woodland at Chidham then crosses fields to reach the harbour shoreline. From here you get fine views across to Thorney Island and down the Thorney Channel. From Prinsted the walk wends its way back past a small orchard and across farmland.

Start Point
The Barleycorn pub on the corner of Cot Lane, Chidham.

By Road
Turn south off the A259 into Cot Lane. There is a small parking area at the top of Cot Lane.

By Bus
Coastliner Service 700, ask for The Barleycorn stop.

By Rail
Nutbourne Railway Station. Walk a few minutes south down Broad Road to reach the start point.

Refreshments
The Barleycorn, Chidham.

Toilets
No public toilets.

Tides
The paths are non-tidal.

Walk Directions
Walk down Cot Lane and turn right into Maybush Copse (1). Take any of the paths across the Copse and eventually you will come to a gate at the far side (2).

Through the gate bear right and follow the path around the field edge. Keep following the footpath signs to turn right and then left and up onto the seawall.

Turn right onto the shoreline path (3) and follow it around the head of the channel. The dark, low buildings on the opposite shore are part of the military buildings on Thorney Island. The marina across the channel is Thornham Marina.

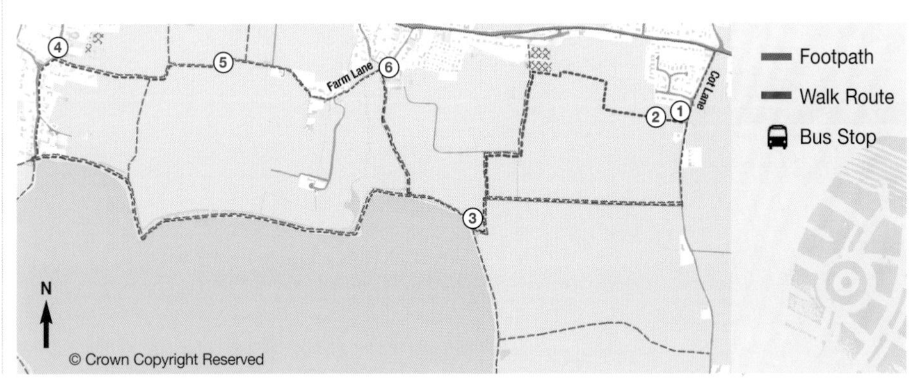

You will eventually come to an open area with lots of benches. Leave the shoreline here to turn inland and take the road to the right of the Southbourne Sea Scouts building.

At The Square, bear right and look carefully for a footpath sign on your right. There is a small wall to climb over. (4)

Keep straight ahead on the footpath which shortly opens out to some fields. Turn left and then follow the path around to the right. After the fields go through the wooden gate (5), the path continues around the edge of a small orchard.

Continue along this path, for a short way it becomes a farm track, then returns to a footpath alongside a brick wall. At the end of this section you will come out into a small area of housing. You are now in Farm Lane.

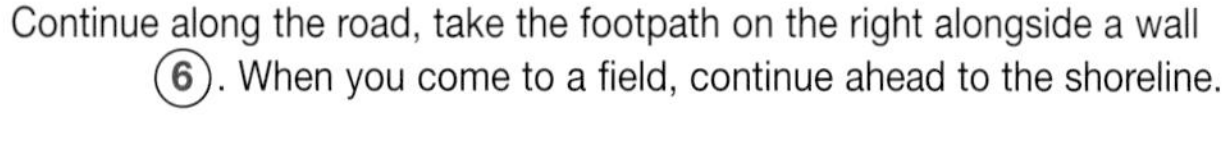

Continue along the road, take the footpath on the right alongside a wall (6). When you come to a field, continue ahead to the shoreline.

At the shoreline path turn left. Take the next footpath on the left (3). You will shortly come to another footpath sign, turn right.

Keep straight ahead to rejoin Cot Lane.
At Cot Lane turn left to return to The Barleycorn.

Maybush Copse

This eight-acre community woodland was purchased in 2009 by the Chichester Harbour Trust with support from the Chichester Harbour Conservancy, the Parish Councils of Southbourne and Chidham and Hambrook, and donations from over 180 local residents. The site was purchased to safeguard the special landscape of the Chichester Harbour Area of Outstanding Natural Beauty, and to create a nature reserve and open space for the community to enjoy.

The site has been planted with 4,500 trees and has a network of woodland paths and a wheelchair path for people to enjoy. There are three beautiful viewpoints with oak benches looking out over the neighbouring farmland towards the Chichester Harbour. In the centre is a wildflower lawn where you are welcome to enjoy a picnic.

Extra Items of Interest

Birds

If you are walking at low tide, look out for these wading birds on the mud.

Curlew

A large wader with very long legs and a down-curved beak. Some arrive in July, stay here until September then travel on. Others stay through the winter months leaving in March.

Oystercatcher

A large black and white bird with bright red legs and beak and a noisy piping call. They don't eat oysters but do feed on shellfish and worms. Usually seen September to February.

Redshank

A delicate-looking wader. Although it is brown, it can be distinguished by its red legs. Nearly 2,000 visit the harbour during the winter months.

Bird photos by George Spraggs

3 | 7.5km/4.5 miles | 2 hours | Map Ref. SU 836 011 - Ordnance Survey Explorer 120

Walk 3

Chichester Marina to Dell Quay

A 7.5km, figure-of-eight walk taking in one the largest marinas in the country and the tiny village of Dell Quay which was once a busy commercial port.

Start Point
Free visitors' car park at Chichester Marina, Birdham.

By Road
From the A27 take the A286 south of Chichester towards the Witterings. After about 2 miles turn right into Chichester Marina. The visitors' car park is the first one you come to on the right.

By Bus
Service 52 or 53 from Chichester to the Witterings. Ask for the Chichester Marina bus stop.

Refreshments
Cafés at Chichester Marina and
The Crown and Anchor at Dell Quay.

Toilets
Near the entrance to Salterns Copse.

Tides
The paths are non-tidal.

Walk Directions
From the bus stop walk down the road towards the Marina where you will shortly find the visitors' car park on your right. From the end of the car park, turn right and pass the barriers with the marina on your left. (1)

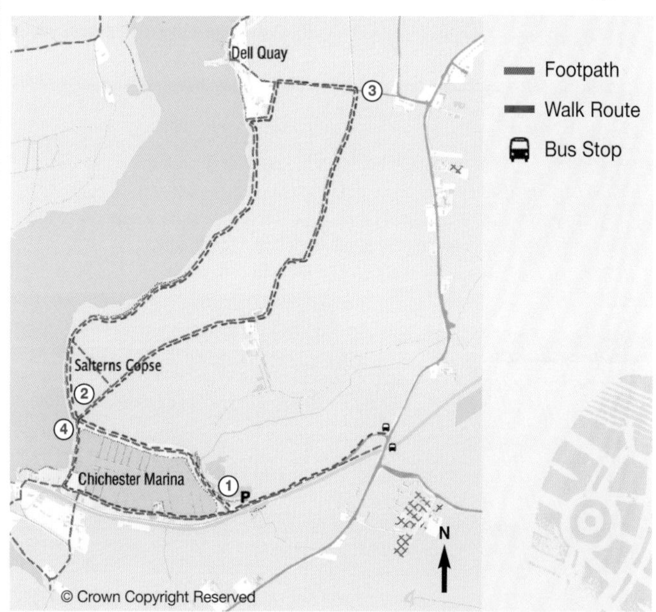

You will pass a large reed bed on your right and then a bird hide. Take a few moments to stop to visit the hide from which you may be able to spot Reed Buntings and Reed Warblers and hear Cetti's Warblers.

Continue down the road to the waterside. In the distance look out for the white roofs of the Goodwood Racecourse grandstand.

When you reach the water, turn right into Salterns Copse and immediately take the left fork. (2) This path follows the shoreline and continues to the edge of the Copse.

The path then continues ahead along a field boundary. You will shortly be able to see the green roof and spire of Chichester Cathedral and the village of Dell Quay.

Continue along the path which eventually turns inland around a garden fence before reaching a road.

Here you can turn left to visit Dell Quay. Walk down the road where you will find The Crown and Anchor, a pub with wonderful harbour views. Past the pub you can walk onto the historic quay which at high tide is likely to be busy with sailing activity.

To continue the walk, return back up the road and past the entrance to the path from which you emerged. Turn right at a wide farm track signposted Apuldram Manor Farm. (3) You are now on a section of the Salterns Way cycle route so please watch out for cyclists.

Follow the farm track which passes between arable fields and then past a cow shed before bearing right to cross a field down to Salterns Copse.

Continue straight ahead alongside the Copse until you reach the entrance.

From here, walk ahead towards the Marina office (4) to cross the lock. If the lock is open you may have to wait a few minutes as boats use it, before the lock keeper closes it for you to cross.

Continue straight ahead towards the canal and then follow the road round to the left with the canal and houseboats on your right.

Make your way across the car park and pick up the path running alongside the Marina. This will take you through a small complex with a café and general store.

The path follows out of the complex and will lead you back to the visitors' car park, or continue on back up the road to the bus stop.

Extra Items of Interest

Salterns Copse
The copse is an eight acre woodland adjacent to the shoreline of Chichester Harbour on Apuldram Manor Farm. It is the largest ancient woodland remnant on the Manhood Peninsula and is of great ecological interest. The area is managed by coppicing. It is divided into ten sections which are coppiced in rotation. Trees such as hazel are cut back to the ground leaving the 'stool' to grow new stems sometimes as many as 30-50.

Chichester Marina
The marina was opened in 1966 with eight pontoons. Further pontoons were added in 1968 and 1970. It can now berth 1071 boats and is the second largest marina in the country.

Chichester Canal
The canal runs from the city of Chichester down to the Harbour, ending at the lock gates by Chichester Yacht Club. It was opened in 1823 as part of a larger canal scheme to carry cargo between London and Portsmouth. Competition from the railways meant that the canal was never commercially viable and it fell into disuse by 1906. A footpath runs alongside the 4km canal and would extend this walk into Chichester. To pick up the path, cross the A286 at the Marina entrance and you will see the canal path opposite you.

Apuldram Airfield
As you walk down the farm track, (3) try to imagine the field on your right as an airfield. Back in February 1943 two runways were laid here to make a temporary airfield. The runways were a metal track which allowed the grass to grow between the steel mesh. This allowed farmers to graze their animals on the airfield when it was not in use. See p68 for more information.

4 | **6km/4 miles** | **2 hours** | **Map Ref. SU 799 013** - Ordnance Survey Explorer 120

Walk 4

Itchenor Circular

This is a 6km walk encircling the harbourside village of Itchenor (also known as West Itchenor). The walk passes through farmland, attractive housing and along the shoreline path with splendid views of the harbour.

Start Point

Bus stop in The Street, Itchenor. This is opposite The Ship Inn and about 100m from the water's edge.

By Road

From the A27 take the A286 south of Chichester towards the Witterings. After about 5 miles, at the small roundabout, continue straight on towards West Wittering. After half a mile take the right hand turn signposted Itchenor. Follow this road for about 2 miles until you see a sign on the left to a pay and display car park. From the car park turn right and then left. You will see the bus stop which is the start point of the walk.

By Bus

Service 150 from Bracklesham and Selsey arrives in Itchenor three times a week. Check the timetable with Compass Travel. Service 53 from Chichester, ask the driver to drop you at the Itchenor Crossroads. You can start the walk at Itchenor Park Farm (4) about 1 mile from the Crossroads bus stop

Refreshments

The Ship Inn, Itchenor.

Toilets

Located at the side of the Harbour Office.

Tides

The shoreline path between point 6 and Itchenor occassionally floods if the tide is higher than 5m.

Walk Directions

From the bus stop opposite the Ship Inn you are almost on the corner of Club Lane (1), walk down the lane to the shoreline.

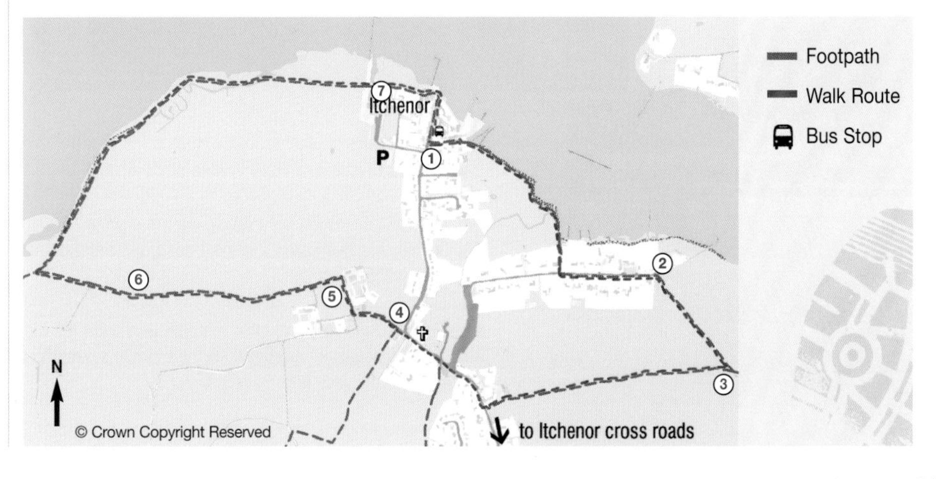

At the shoreline turn right and continue along the path which eventually turns inland between a wall and a hedge before joining Spinney Lane. Turn left along Spinney Lane and walk to the end of the road. Just past a small turning area, take the footpath to your right through a gate (2).

To your right is an open field and on the left a small woodland which gives way to an open field with views to the water.

Walk to the field edge then turn right, almost back on yourself (3), following the footpath sign to walk along the field boundary. The hedge is on your left.

3

Keep following the path between two fields heading towards some farm buildings.

Pass the buildings and keep going straight ahead with a fence on your right and then over a plank bridge to the road.

At the road, turn right. Watch out for traffic on this section. You will pass the village pond on your left and a church on your right.

Shortly after the church take the road on your left signposted to Itchenor Park House and Farm (4).

After a short way turn right following the sign 'All Farm Traffic'. After a few yards the footpath goes behind the cobbled wall (5).

Continue along the path, over the stile and then turn left. Keep straight on along the concrete road passing a cricket field on your left.

Extra Items of Interest

Photo by George Spraggs

Little Egrets
These bright white birds look like small herons. They only started coming here in the 1990s, previously they spent most of their time further south in Mediterranean countries. Chichester Harbour now has the second largest colony of Little Egrets in the UK with over 250 in 2006. In the harbour they can be seen on marshy fields near the shoreline as well as on the intertidal area.

Itchenor Park Farm
Look out for the red brick farm bulding. This was originally the carriage house to the country house called Itchenor Park. One of Charles II's descendants, Charles Lennox, Duke of Richmond, bought Itchenor Park and established a farm here. Evidence of this can be seen by the Royal coat of arms on two of the farm buildings. The first you may see is dated 1783 and the second, dated 1778, is closest to the farm wall. Charles II gave Itchenor House to one of his mistresses. Charles also had other, more nautical connections with Itchenor. His Royal Yacht, Fubs, (also reputed to be the nickname of his mistress), was based at Itchenor.

Chichester Harbour Conservancy
At the end of the walk you will pass the Harbour Office, the base for Chichester Harbour Conservancy. The Conservancy was established in 1971. It is in the unique position of being both the harbour authority and responsible for managing the Area of Outstanding Natural Beauty.

The road becomes a mud track. Keep going until you see a squeeze gate in the fence on your right (6).

This path takes you back to Itchenor. There are a number of benches on this path to rest and enjoy the views.

Along the path are ancient oak trees. This type of wooded shoreline is typical of Chichester Harbour. After a while on your right is a marshy area where you are likely to see Little Egrets.

You will come to a section of metalled path which has been laid for wheelchair users to have access to a harbour viewpoint.

Just before the boatyard, there is a footpath on the right signposted to The Car Park (7). This will take you directly back to your car. Alternatively, continue straight ahead crossing the boatyard and take the small path ahead of you which will come out at Haines Boatyard and the Harbour Office. From here turn right to take you back to the start point.

5 | **7.5km/4.5 miles** | **2.5 hours** | **Map Ref. SZ 780 985** - Ordnance Survey Explorer 120

Walk 5

West Wittering to Itchenor Circular

This walk starts in the pretty village of West Wittering, following a little used lane down to the shoreline. From the shoreside footpath there are fine views across to Bosham and the South Downs. The second half of the walk passes through a farm and across fields to complete the circuit. The walk is 7.5km or if you take the extended route into Itchenor it is 8.5km.

Start Point
Old House at Home pub, Pound Road, West Wittering PO20 8AD.

By Road
Take the A286 towards Witterings and follow signs for West Wittering Beach. Park in Rookwood Road near the Old House at Home pub.

By Bus
Service 53 Chichester to the Witterings. Bus stops on both sides of the road near the Old House at Home.

Refreshments
Cafés and a pub at West Wittering or if you take the extended walk, The Ship Inn at Itchenor.

Toilets
In Pound Road, West Wittering or at Itchenor for the extended walk.

Tides
The path between points 2 and 3 floods if the tide is higher than 4.5m. Start the walk at least an hour before or after high tide.

Walk Directions
From the Old House at Home in Rookwood Road, look for the large brown signs to West Wittering Beach on the corner of Pound Road. Turn into Pound Road and take the first right – Ellanore Lane (1). This is a little used lane which leads down to the shoreline.

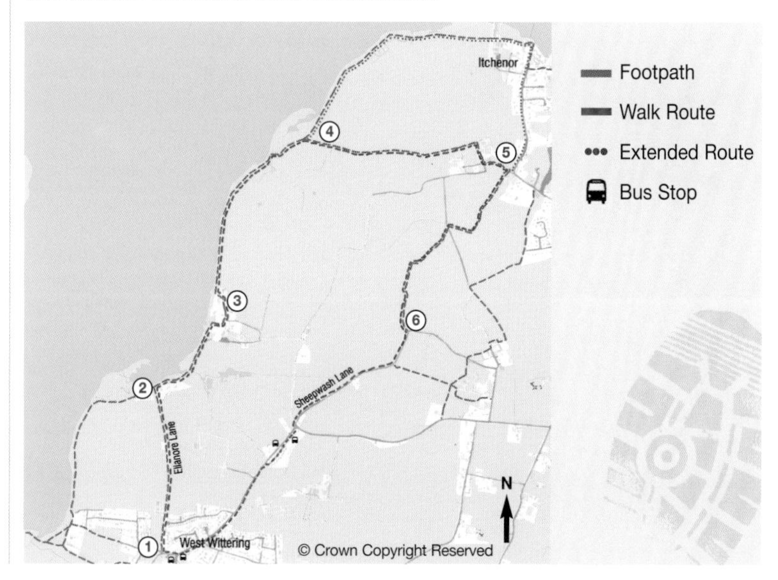

At the end of the lane go through the gate (2) straight ahead of you and bear right onto the shoreline path.

After a while the path turns inland, then left through a small area of housing. Follow the footpath signs and then through a kissing gate (3) to take you back to the shoreline.

Continue along the path, looking out for the Spinnaker Tower at Portsmouth and further along Bosham Church in the distance. Eventually you will pass a pond on your right – Horse Pond. Keep going for a few more minutes, as you come into a wooded area, take the footpath to your right (4) through a squeeze gate.

Extended Route

If you want to continue into Itchenor then instead of turning right keep following the shoreline, crossing the boatyard and then coming out by the Harbour Office. Turn right up the road, passing The Ship Inn.

*Continue up the road, watching out for traffic. As you approach the village hall, turn right through the white gates and then take the footpath immediately to your left. Continue the route from *.*

At the end of the path, go through another squeeze gate and bear left up the track which becomes a concrete road.

Just before you reach the farm buildings, turn right following the footpath over a stile, with a low cobbled barn on your left. The path then bears left through a gap in the wall. Continue on and then left at the crossroads.

*(*Extended route – rejoin here)*
Just before the white gates turn right to pick up the footpath. If you reach the village hall you have gone too far.

5

Follow this path across fields until you reach the farm road. The path to your left is the Salterns Way cycle route.

6

Cross over the farm road and follow the footpath over two fields (5), this section can be very muddy, until you come out onto Sheepwash Lane (6). Turn right and keep going until you come to Rookwood Road. Note this section of Sheepwash Lane is shared with the Salterns Way cycle route.

At Rookwood Road turn right. If you are getting the bus back, you will shortly see bus stops on both sides of the road. If not continue along, taking care as it can be a busy road. You will pass some shops and the village hall and then you are back at your car.

Extra Items of Interest

Saltmarsh
If you are walking with the tide partially out you will see saltmarsh especially when you first come onto the shoreline from Ellanore Lane. Saltmarsh is found on the upper part of the intertidal area. It is made up of plants that can cope with being regularly under saltwater. Different types of plants grow at different levels. Nearer the deepwater channel there is Glasswort and Common Cordgrass. Towards the land, Saltmarsh Grass and the purple flowered Thrift and Sea Lavender grow. The saltmarsh is at its most colourful between June–August.

Measured Half Mile
Walking along the shore look out for two tall posts in the water with a cross on top. These are one end of the 'measured half mile'. Out of season, motorboats can get permission to test their engines in this area of the harbour. When they line up the crosses on the two posts they are at the start of the half mile which finishes when they pass the second set of lined up posts.

6 | **6km/4 miles** | **1.5 hours** | **Map Ref. SZ 780 985** - Ordnance Survey Explorer 120

Walk 6

West Wittering Beach & East Head

A 6km walk along the sandy beach of West Wittering and around the sand dunes of East Head with far-reaching views across to the Isle of Wight and then back past the old Coastguard cottages and church. This walk is good at anytime of the year but avoid sunny, summer weekends when up to 15,000 people come down to the beach.

Start Point
Old House at Home pub, Rookwood Road, West Wittering PO20 8AD.

By Road
Take the A286 towards Witterings and follow signs for West Wittering. Park in Rookwood Road near the Old House at Home pub. Alternatively you can park in the beach car park (daily charge) and begin the walk from there. Please note this road is very busy on hot, summer days.

By Bus
Service 52 or 53 Chichester to the Witterings. Bus stops on both sides of the road near the Old House at Home.

Refreshments
Cafés and a pub at West Wittering and a café in the beach car park.

Toilets
In Pound Road and in the beach car park.

Tides
The walk is most enjoyable at low tide when large expanses of sand are revealed. East Head is on tidal sands. When the tide is 4.6m or higher it is possible to walk through the dunes instead.

Walk Directions
From the Old House at Home in Rookwood Road, look for the large brown signs to West Wittering Beach on the corner of Pound Road. Turn into Pound Road (1). On your left are public toilets, immediately past these bear left (2) and follow the road down to the car park entrance.

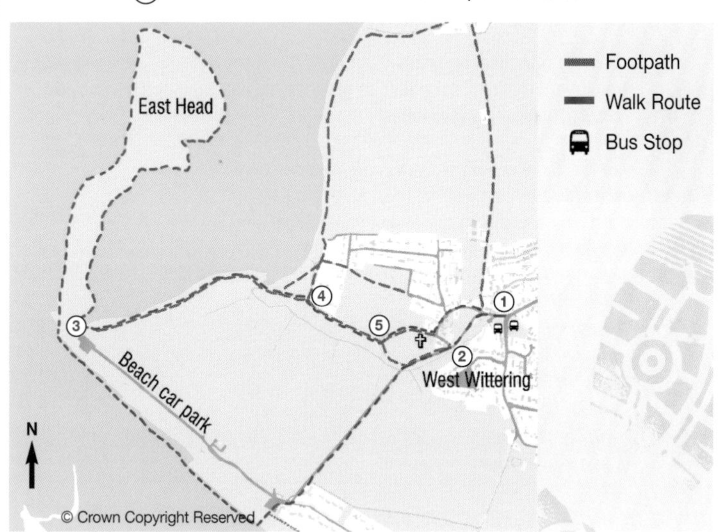

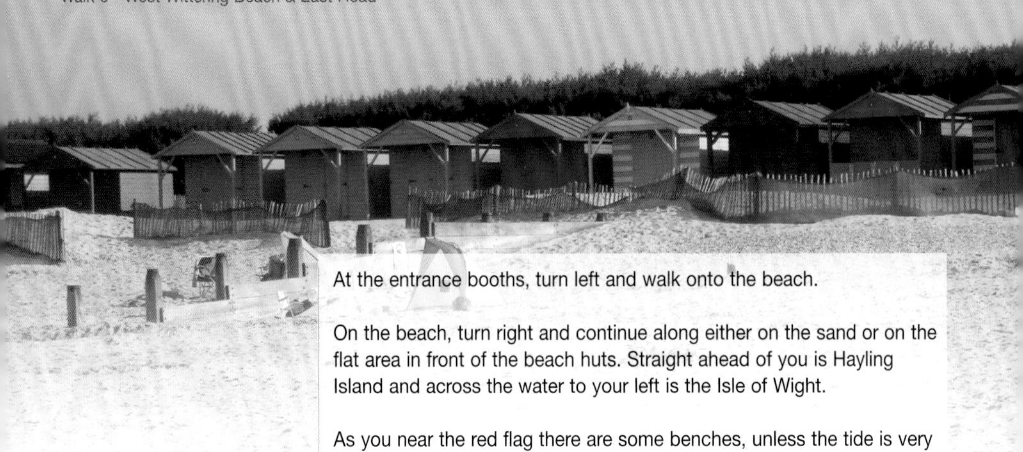

At the entrance booths, turn left and walk onto the beach.

On the beach, turn right and continue along either on the sand or on the flat area in front of the beach huts. Straight ahead of you is Hayling Island and across the water to your left is the Isle of Wight.

As you near the red flag there are some benches, unless the tide is very low, you will need to walk on the upper shingle area to get around the corner onto East Head.

Follow the beach around the sand dune spit. Depending on the wind, you may prefer to walk around the spit in an anti-clockwise direction.

If you do go into the dunes, please avoid trampling on Marram Grass and please stay out of the fenced or roped off areas.

When you have completed the circuit of East Head, finish on the land side. Head towards the car park but rather than going into it, follow the footpath round to the left (3). If the tide is high you can take the path alongside the low fence, or continue along the shoreline. This is a tidal path and can be squelchy.

Either way you will join the path on top of the sea wall. You will come to an open grassy area called Snowhill. There are a number of benches here to rest and enjoy the view.

Bear right across the grass. Turn right along the lane (4). You will pass a row of old Coastguard cottages on your left and then come to a wide gravelled drive on your left (5).

Follow the footpath signs through a small caravan park, through a gate and then across a field and over a wall into the churchyard. Take time to visit St Peter & St Paul Church.

Bear left across the churchyard which will bring you into Pound Road. Turn left with the school on your right and continue back to your start point.

Shell Guide

As you walk along look out for these common shells.

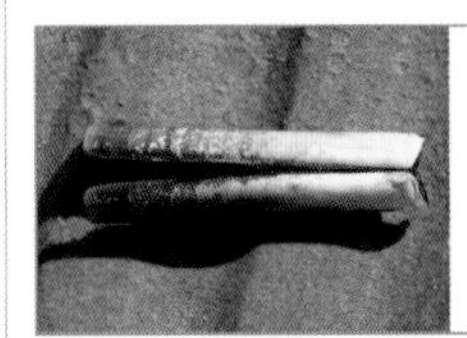

Razor
A common burrowing mollusc. It burrows vertically into the sand leaving a small hole through which it feeds.

Common Whelk
Pretty, whorled shell which is popular with children. Whelks are carnivorous and can live for up to 10 years.

Common Cockle
This cockle is eaten by both man and birds such as Oystercatchers.

Slipper Limpet
These were accidentally introduced into Britain from the United States in the late 1800s.

Native Oyster
These are bi-valve which means 'two shells'. Oysters change their sex depending on the temperature of the water.

Common Mussel
This edible mussel is found in shallow water attached to stones. They may live up to 15 years or more, and produce their young 'spats' during spring/early summer.

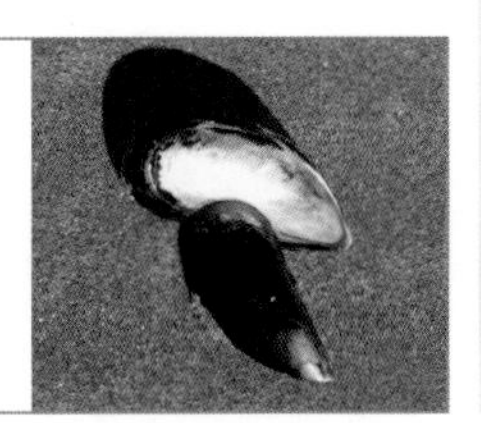

Extra Items of Interest

East Head
East Head is an important sand dune feature at the entrance to Chichester Harbour. The dunes are owned by the National Trust and are designated as a Site of Special Scientific Interest (SSSI).

West Wittering Estate
In 1951 the Church Commissioners, who owned all the land between the harbour entrance and East Wittering, were in discussion with Butlins and another similar organisation with a view to selling the land for a holiday complex. As a result the West Wittering Estate Company was set up by local residents. They purchased the land for £20,546.14s9d to preserve it for public enjoyment and to protect the rural and undeveloped nature of the area. The car park has been run commercially since the 1920s and provides many facilities.

Sir Henry Royce
On Rookwood Road look for the Sir Henry Royce plaque. Sir Henry lived and worked in West Wittering from 1917 until his

death. Some of his greatest designs were carried out at his nearby studio. In 2003 Rolls Royce opened a plant at Goodwood, Chichester which now produces its range of luxury cars for export around the world.

7	7.5km/4.5 miles	2 hours	Map Ref. SU 719 047 - Ordnance Survey Explorer 120

Walk 7
Northney Explorer

Having crossed the busy bridge onto Hayling Island you soon reach the tranquillity of Northney. The 12th century church with its pretty churchyard makes a pleasant midway resting spot before continuing through farmland for a short stretch along the shoreline.

Start Point
The Ship pub, Langstone PO9 1RD.

By Road
There is a free public car park at The Ship which is on the left just before the bridge onto Hayling Island.

By Bus
Service 30/31 from Havant to Hayling Island stops at The Ship.

Refreshments
The Ship and The Royal Oak, Langstone and Northney Farm Tea Rooms.

Toilets
In the car park at Langstone.

Tides
The paths are non-tidal.

Walk Directions
Cross the bridge onto Hayling Island (1). Although this is a busy and noisy start to the walk it is the only place with views across both Langstone and Chichester Harbours. Please watch out for cyclists on this section.

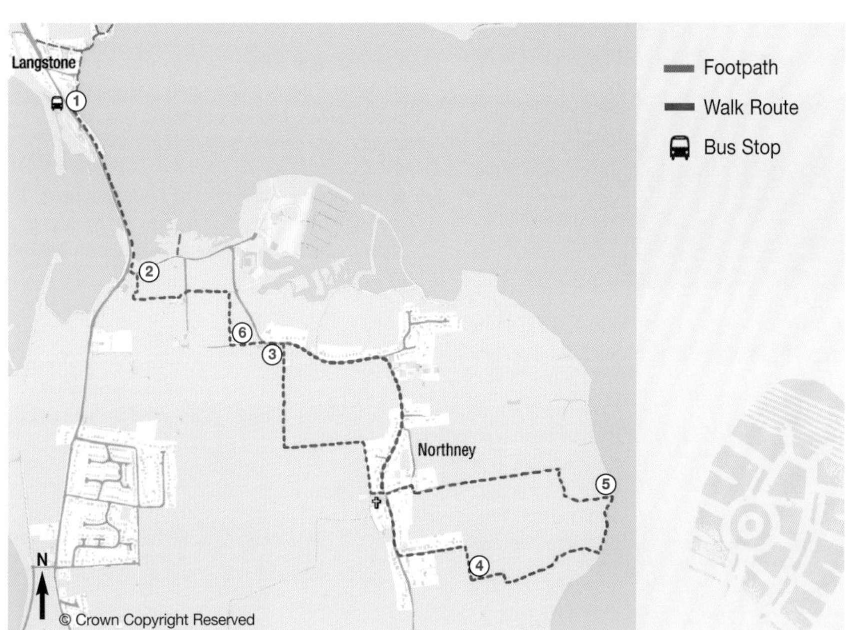

Turn left into Northney Road and then immediately right onto the footpath towards the petrol station. Keep alongside the hedge which brings you out at a small parking area. Look for the footpath on the left and go over the stile (2).

Keep straight ahead following the footpath as it turns left, eventually coming out at the road.

Turn right onto the road and watch out for traffic on this short stretch. You will soon see a footpath to the right (3). This is just before the recreation ground and opposite the village name sign.

Take this path, it turns left and then right before coming out at St Peters Church. There are a couple of benches here if you want a rest.

Continue straight across the churchyard and through a wooden gate. The path passes behind some houses and then reaches the road. Turn right and then shortly left into St Peters Avenue.

At the end of the Avenue, turn right and after a few minutes take the footpath on your left. (4)

Turn right and follow the field edge to the shoreline. This is private land opened to the public by the landowner. Please keep dogs under close control on this section.

At the shoreline take time to enjoy the views. To your right is the Harbour entrance, opposite is Thorney Island and to the left Emsworth backed by the South Downs.

Turn right along the path and when you reach the wooden fence across the path, turn left down the steps (5) leaving the Harbour behind you.

Continue ahead around the field edge, then through a wooden gate and onto a wide track. This comes out at Church Lane with its pretty cottages and houses. You will come out opposite the church.

Here you can either retrace your steps by walking to the far right of the church car park to pick up the footpath, to go to Northney Farm Tea Rooms, turn right and continue along the road. The tea rooms are on the right. Once you are refreshed continue along the road which bears left and becomes Northney Road.

When the road bends to the right, take the track straight ahead (6) and then retrace your steps back to Langstone.

Extra Items of Interest

Church of St Peter's

The church of St Peter's was built by monks of the Abbey of Jumieges, Normandy, in 1140, close to the site of an Iron Age shrine, later the site of a Roman temple. Some of St Peter's interior pillars stand on roughly hewn stones taken from the Roman temple. The delightful church interior, little changed since 1250, is best appreciated sitting quietly in the back pew, some say in the peaceful presence of the ghost of a sailor, drowned whilst crossing the Wadeway in a storm. A 21st century extension, tacked on to the west door in the shape of an upturned boat, sits in surprising harmony with the remainder of the church. Princess Catherine Yourievsky is buried to the right of the path leading to the 13th century north door. An escapee from the Bolshevik revolution, she found peace in Northney for the latter part of her life.

Martin Rhodes

Coastal Grazing Marsh

The fields by the shoreline are an increasingly rare habitat – coastal grazing marsh. Historically grazing animals have been used to manage land close to the harbour. However, in recent years beef cattle numbers have been declining as the cost of production increases and the financial returns fall. This farm is in the 'Three Harbours Beef' Scheme. All the animals in the scheme are reared on either Hampshire or Sussex coastal plains. They are reared on their mother's milk and grass for the first six months and then spend two summers on the flower-rich grazing marshes.

Keeping the marshes grazed is essential for internationally important species of birds such as Lapwings, Redshank and Brent Geese. In addition it encourages the growth of Southern Marsh orchids. The beef is sold through local farmshops and direct to the public.

See www.threeharboursbeef.co.uk

8 | **13.5km/8.5 miles** | **4 hours** | **Map Ref. SU 752 057** - Ordnance Survey Explorer 120

Walk 8

Thorney Island Circular

This is the ideal walk for those who love sea views. Doing the walk clockwise from Emsworth gets the inland sections over at the beginning. Once onto the shoreline, the route is very easy to follow so you can concentrate on enjoying the route rather than reading instructions. A visit to the Church is a must as is looking out for many of the birds that thrive in this tranquil area.

Start Point
The Lord Raglan pub, Queen Street, Emsworth.

By Road
Emsworth. There are a number of pay and display car parks in Emsworth. Allow at least 5 hours for the walk. Alternatively, there is a small parking area on the corner of Thorney Road and Thornham Lane. If parking here follow the directions from the fourth paragraph.

By Bus
Emsworth. Coastliner Service 700 stops at Hermitage Bridge which is very close to the start point.

Refreshments
Numerous restaurants, pubs and cafés at Emsworth, Boaters Café at Thornham Marina and The Deck at Emsworth Marina. There are no refreshments on Thorney Island, take your own drinks and snacks.

Toilets
In the South Street car park, Emsworth.

Tides
The path floods between points 1 and 2 and near the church at point 6 when the tide is 5m or higher

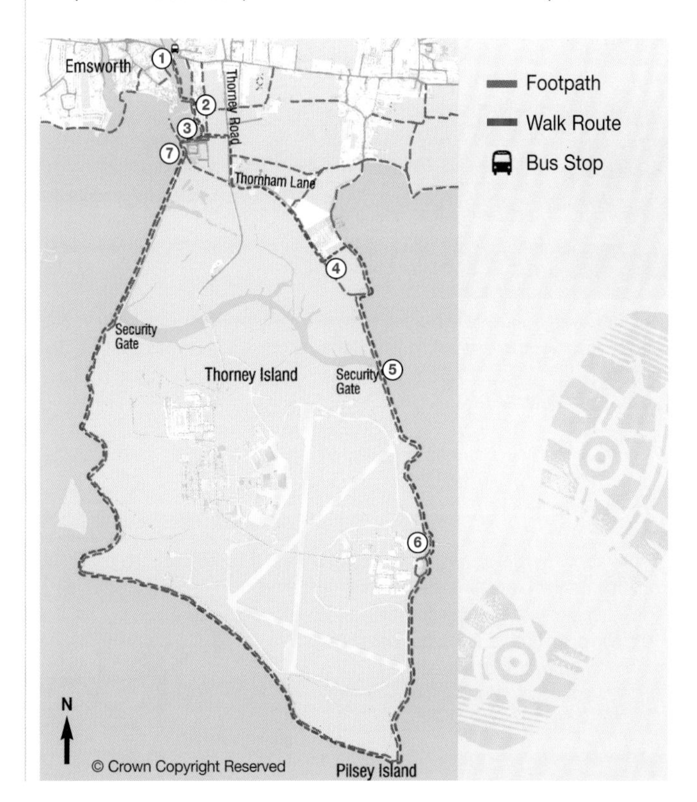

Walk Directions

Take the footpath alongside the Lord Raglan pub and through Chequers Quay. Go under the arch and through a gate onto the path alongside Slipper Mill Pond. (1)

At the end of the pond, go through the gate and then turn right in front of the converted mill building. Continue ahead through the boatyard (2). Watch out for moving machinery.

Turn right in front of the first few 'stilt' houses, then left and then right at the next footpath sign along Osprey Quay. Look out for the footpath on the left across a field (3). There are usually horses in this field.

At the road, turn right and then shortly left into Thornham Lane. Just past Thornham Marina (look out for the big whale!) there are some large rocks across the road (4).

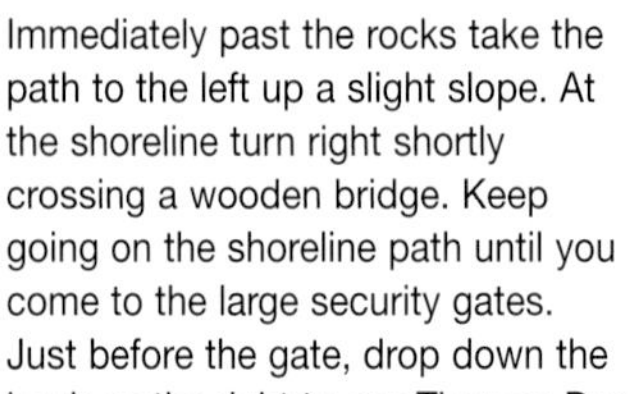

Immediately past the rocks take the path to the left up a slight slope. At the shoreline turn right shortly crossing a wooden bridge. Keep going on the shoreline path until you come to the large security gates. Just before the gate, drop down the bank on the right to see Thorney Deeps. This was once part of the Chichester Ship Canal.

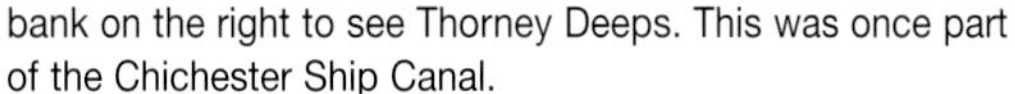

At the gates (5) press the buzzer. You will usually be let straight through but on occasion you will be asked your name, address and purpose of visit. Do not be put off, this is a formality as the land past the gate is owned by the Ministry of Defence.

Once on Thorney Island do not stray off the clearly marked path. Call the Guard Post on 01243 388269 or the Guard Room on 01243 388275 if you get into difficulty.

After about a mile you will pass a dinghy park. Just beyond, the path climbs up the bank towards the 13th century church of St Nicholas (6). Take time to visit the church which is usually open. There are some benches in the churchyard for a break.

If the tide is low continue along the beach in front of the Thorney Island Sailing Club (TISC). If the path is flooded here, turn right before the club building, then left following the signs for the high water footpath to return to the shoreline.

At the tip of the island you will see the sandy beach and dunes of Pilsey Island. This area is leased by the RSPB and is important for nesting and roosting birds. There is no public access from the footpath.

After a while you will come to a bird hide which is a good spot for a break on a windy or wet day.

As you walk up the west side of the island, look out for seals on the mudflats if the tide is low.

At the security gates you will be asked your name and then let through. Here you can either continue along the shoreline path or drop down the bank on the right to walk alongside the Deeps. Either way the paths rejoin.

Take the path in front of the 'stilt' houses (7) and then turn right at the marina. If you have parked at the road junction keep going to Thorney Road and then turn right.

Otherwise turn left at the next set of houses. Retrace your steps back through the marina and around the Slipper Mill Pond to return to the start point.

Extra Items of Interest

St Nicholas Church

This 13th century church was described by AA Evans in the Chichester Diocesan Gazette as the 'loneliest, remotest, last seen, least known and altogether utmost church in Sussex'. This description still rings true today. The pretty church is still used by local parishioners but is inaccessible to the general public other than via the footpath or by yachtsmen landing at the nearby jetty. Despite its age there are a number of modern touches including an engraved window and a slate pulpit. In the well kept churchyard, RAF graves lie alongside the graves of Germans who lost their lives here during the Second World War.

Seals

Around 25 Harbour Seals regularly visit Chichester Harbour. Each one has unique markings and even their colourings can be different ranging from tan to grey, black and brown. The females are generally smaller but with a longer lifespan. This is the only known rookery in the Eastern English Channel and so they are considered regionally unique and therefore very important. These seals forage in the Eastern Solent, between Southampton and Selsey Bill, often in Chichester and Langstone harbours, and regularly cross to the Isle of Wight.

Photo by Meryl Mead-Briggs

9	16km/10 miles	5 hours	Map Ref. SU 806 039 - Ordnance Survey Explorer 120

Walk 9
Two Villages and a Ferry

A 16km walk starting in the historic village of Bosham. Cutting across the peninsula, the route passes through reedbeds to a traditionally managed meadow. Heading down the Fishbourne Channel, the route takes in the tiny village of Dell Quay and passes through two marinas before arriving at Itchenor for the ferry crossing across the channel.

Start Point
Bosham pay & display car park.

Ferry
Please note the ferry is seasonal, to confirm the running times please call 07970 378350. Out of season you will not be able to complete this walk. Usually the ferry running times are 0900-1800, daily from mid-May to the end of September. Weekends and bank holidays only from April to mid-May and through October.

By Road
Turn south off the A259 towards Bosham. Follow the signs to the pay & display car park.

By Bus
Service 56 between Chichester and Bosham. This is an hourly service running Monday to Saturdays but not on bank holidays. Please check for up to date details. The bus stop is in the car park.

Refreshments
Tea shops and a pub in Bosham. The Crown & Anchor pub at Dell Quay, cafés at Chichester Marina and The Ship at Itchenor.

Toilets
In the car park at Bosham, side of the Harbour Office Itchenor and at Chichester Marina.

Tides
The path between the ferry and Bosham is tidal and floods when the tide is 4.7m or higher. The walk can be completed at high tide but you will need to take the inland route straight up from the ferry path to the road.

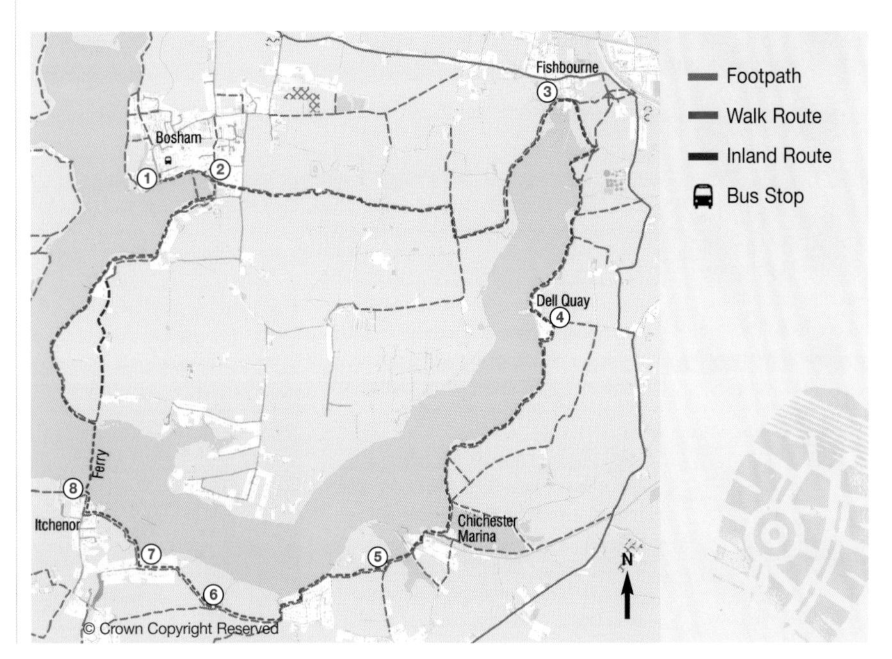

Walk Directions

Walk out of Bosham car park and turn left. Just before the water take the path on the left between two houses (1) and continue on this path towards the head of the channel.

Pass Harbour Road on your left and a couple of houses to reach a grassy triangle. Bear left and take the footpath ahead of you (2) between two houses. (If you reach Old School House you have gone too far.)

Cross the road and continue straight ahead. The path turns right and then left and passes by an isolated house before reaching another road. Cross over and continue ahead.

At the end of the tree-lined path, turn right and then shortly left. Keep going and before long you will see Fishbourne Channel. As you head towards the shoreline bear left following the path through an area of oak trees. The path then goes up a couple of steps and continues on the field edge.

After a while you will reach some steps down to the reedbeds (3), eventually coming out by Fishbourne Mill Pond. Cross the road and carry on the path through the metal kissing gate.

At the meadows, bear right to cross a bridge and go through a kissing gate. Continue to the next footpath junction. Here you can either bear left or continue ahead which is a slightly longer route. Both paths join again at the other side of the field.

Please note
Chichester District Council have a Dogs on Lead by Direction Order covering the head of the Fishbourne Channel. This prevents disturbance to sensitive wildlife.

Continue along the path through a series of kissing gates to reach Dell Quay. The path comes out by The Crown and Anchor. If you want to explore the small quay turn right here.

Otherwise, turn left walking up the road away from the harbour. After a few houses there is a footpath on the right (4). Keep going along the field edge and then alongside a woodland to reach Chichester Marina.

Walk towards the Marina office and cross over the lock. If it is open, wait patiently and the lock keeper will close it for you to cross. Once across the lock, walk straight ahead, when you reach the canal turn right and then left to cross the old lock gates.

Continue through the narrow path, then turn right through another narrow path. At the road, cross over and continue ahead to Birdham Pool.

Once through the marina bear left and past a big house, take the footpath down a small lane on the right (5). The path bears left on the right hand side of a field and then in front of the gardens of some harbourside properties.

The path turns inland to reach a residential road. Turn right. At the road junction turn right and keep going down a concrete road towards Westlands Farm.

Before the farm buildings turn left and go through the gate on the right (6). Keep ahead across a couple of fields and alongside a small woodland to reach Spinney Lane. Turn left.

After about 300m there is a footpath (7) on the right taking you back to the shoreline. When you reach the sailing club, turn left. You will come out opposite The Ship.

Turn right and walk down to the Harbour Office. Turn left past the office and down the public jetty (8) to catch the ferry. The ferry is usually berthed on the left of the jetty head. If it is not there wait and it will be back shortly. As well as taking people across the water it takes people to and from their moored boats.

Once off the ferry, walk up to the footpath. If it is low tide turn left and continue around the shoreline route to a road.

If it is high tide, continue straight ahead up a small path and then bear left at the road which will come out at the same place as the shoreline walk.

Continue around the road, or there is a higher footpath if the tide is in, towards the head of the channel. If it is low tide you can shortcut across the Wadeway. Otherwise continue around the top of the channel and retrace your steps back to the car park or bus stop.

Extra Items of Interest

Fishbourne Reed Beds
Walking through the reeds that are taller than you and hearing the birds sing and the wind rustle the leaves is a magical experience. The reeds growing in this bed are the Common Reed. They are Britain's tallest native grass. The beds are an important habitat for Reed Warblers and Sedge Warblers that come here from Africa to breed.

Smuggling
Smuggling is reported to have been rife in the Dell Quay area. Goods were dropped off all around the harbour, in particular at Copperas Point. Contraband was stored in Salterns Copse to hide it from the Customs Officers, before it was collected and taken inland. The Sussex County Magazine in 1927 reports a 'perfectly true incident', which happened at the Quay in the early part of the 19th century. A French yacht with flag at half-mast arrived at the Quay and was met by a hearse and mourners. A weighty coffin was solemnly unloaded and was over the Downs before the Customs officers realised it was full of smuggled goods.

Taken from Chichester Harbour – A Reference Guide

10	8km/5 miles	2.5 hours	Map Ref. SU 794 035 - Ordnance Survey Explorer 120

Walk 10
Chidham Circular

An 8km circular walk with some of the best panoramic views of the harbour. There is always something to watch on the water, whether it is groups of young people learning to sail or kayak, or birds diving for fish.

Start Point
Cobnor Farm Amenity car park.

By Road
From the A259 turn south onto Chidham Lane. Keep on this road signposted towards Chidham East. After a mile turn left into the Amenity car park. If you reach the sign for Cobnor House you have gone too far.

Refreshments
The Old House at Home.

Tides
The shoreline section to the southwest floods when the tide is 4.5m or higher. Aim to reach it two hours before or after high tide.

Walk Directions
Take the first path on the left out of the car park. Going up a few steps you can see Bosham Church in the distance (1). Turn to the right and then left along the field edge, heading towards the shoreline.

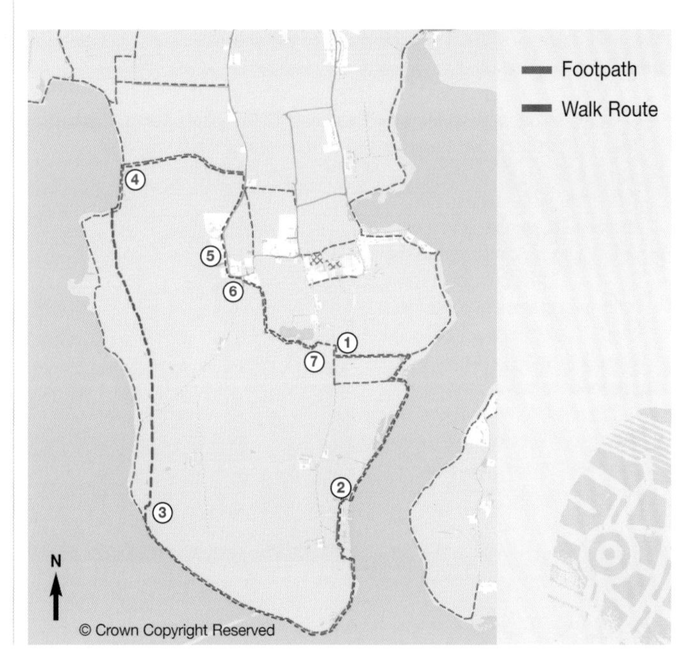

At the shoreline path, turn right and keep going. Just before you reach the big accommodation boat for Christian Youth Enterprises (2), the path turns inland.

Carefully follow the footpath signs around the buildings and activity fields of the two sailing centres. You will shortly come onto a hard surfaced path through a dinghy park.

The path then turns left towards the shoreline. This section is suitable for wheelchairs. It was opened in 1988 on land kindly donated by Martin Beale, whose family still live at Cobnor House.

Keep on the path, there are a number of benches along this route for a break and to enjoy the view. The path eventually leads down a few steps to the shoreline. Turn right along the shore.

Once you have passed the shoreline oaks, climb back up onto the bank. Take the footpath that heads inland to the right of the fence (3).

When the path reaches the shoreline, turn right and look out for the footpath sign to the right (4). The path goes down a few steps and turns back on itself. Turn left at the field edge to walk inland across fields.

At the road, turn right. You will shortly come to some houses and then the Old House at Home pub (5).

5

Past the pub the road bears to the left. Take time to visit the church and look out for their collection of historical 'teasel people'. Just before the church there is a footpath on the right (6).

Keep on this wide grassy path as it wiggles around fields. On the straight section with electricity poles look out for the small unsigned path on the left (7) leading back to the road.

Turn right to return to the car park.

Extra Items of Interest

Coastal Realignment

On the western side you will see a line of low, crossed stakes. These are the remains of an unsuccessful land reclamation scheme in the 19th century. The island that has formed over some of the stakes is now a major wader roost in winter and in summer is sometimes used by breeding terns.

On the eastern side, land is being returned to the sea to create mudflat and saltmarsh habitats. This is the area to your right as you walk along the wheelchair accessible path. Two breaches have been created in the sea wall to allow water circulation and drainage. Over time four hectares of intertidal habitat will be created. This type of land is favoured by wading birds for feeding. In addition new water vole habitats are being created to ensure their continued presence on the site.

11 | 7km/4 miles | 2 hours | Map Ref. SU 858 048 - Ordnance Survey Explorer 120

Walk 11

Chichester to Bosham

A 7km walk starting in the heart of the Cathedral city of Chichester. The route leads through the urban outskirts of the city quickly reaching the Chichester Harbour Area of Outstanding Natural Beauty. Crossing meadows and fields, the walk takes in a section of the shoreline as it reaches the ancient village of Bosham. This walk can be extended by following Walk 12 Across the Harbour.

Start Point
Chichester Cathedral, West Street, Chichester.

By Road
There are a number of car parks in Chichester.

By Bus
Bus stops in West Street serve most of the routes into the City including the 700 Coastliner. The stops are very close to the Cathedral. The return bus from Bosham to Chichester is Service 56. This is an hourly service running Monday to Saturdays but not on Bank Holidays. Please check for up to date details.

By Rail
From Chichester station walk north towards the Cross and then turn left into West Street, the Cathedral is on your left.

Refreshments
Lots of pubs, restaurants and cafés in Chichester. In Bosham there are two teashops and a pub.

Toilets
In Tower Street, Chichester opposite the Cathedral and in Bosham car park.

Tides
The path through the reedbeds just after point 4 floods when the tide is 4.8m or higher.

Walk Directions
From the Cathedral walk west along West Street (1) away from the main shopping area. At the roundabout cross over and continue straight ahead into Westgate. Cross over a mini roundabout into the final section of Westgate. At the end bear right and cross the railway line using the footbridge.

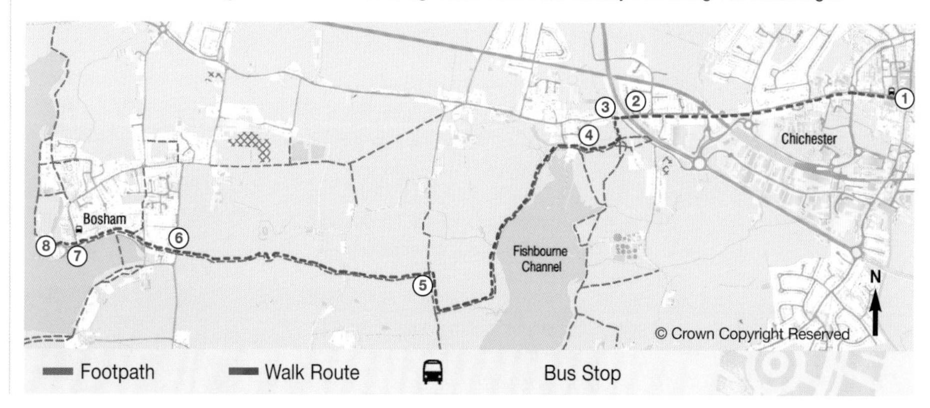

Bear to the right and continue on. There is pedestrian access on the left into Tesco if you need picnic supplies. At the end of the road go through the underpass (2) - the A27 is now above you! Once through turn left and then cross the road at the crossing point for bicycles and pedestrians.

Turn right and walk past a couple of houses. Look out for the footpath to the left through a kissing gate (3). Cross over a small stream and then into Fishbourne Meadows. Turn right.

Cows often graze these meadows, if they are in the way approach them slowly and they will move away. Please keep your dog on a lead through the meadows.

As the path enters the second meadow, bear right to walk alongside the stream. Cross over the first bridge.

After the bridge, bear to the right, then left to go through a metal kissing gate (4).

Continue along by a small section of the stream, then through another gate to bring you out by the Mill Pond.

Continue along the footpath straight ahead of you. The path shortly passes through a large reedbed and then up some steps. Turn left and follow the path down the side of the Fishbourne Channel.

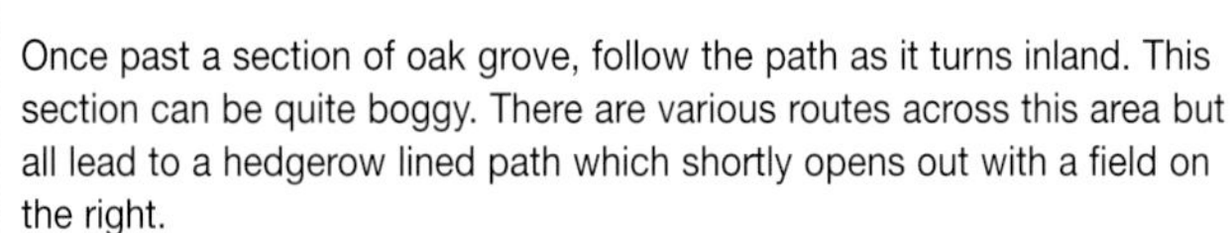

Once past a section of oak grove, follow the path as it turns inland. This section can be quite boggy. There are various routes across this area but all lead to a hedgerow lined path which shortly opens out with a field on the right.

When you get to the field junction, turn left and continue to the metalled lane. Turn right and continue along to the junction with a road. Turn right.

At the entrance to Old Park Farm, there is a clear view of the Cathedral across the fields to the right.

Continue ahead looking out for the footpath to the left (5) which leads across to Bosham.

As you near some houses, the path turns right and then left before reaching the road. Cross over the road and the path continues alongside the flint cottage (6). At the end of the path, cross over the grass bank then follow the path to the right into the village of Bosham. If it is low tide you can walk along the shore road. If you take this road, at Bosham Lane (7) turn right and then immediately left.

Alternatively if you have taken the footpath in front of the houses, cross straight over Bosham Lane (7) and continue ahead. This road leads to the Church.

Having visited the Church (8), continue through the churchyard to come out to Quay Meadow, an area of grassland managed by the National Trust with harbour views that is ideal for picnics.

When you are ready to get the bus back or if you are continuing to walk 12, return to Bosham Lane. Follow signs to the car park where you will find the bus stop and public toilets.

Extra Items of Interest

Holy Trinity Church, Bosham

The church was built around AD1050-1100, although there were later additions and alterations particularly in the 12th and 13th centuries. Parts of the church can be dated very accurately using tree ring dating. The spire, for example, is built of timbers felled in the winter of 1405/06 and the summer of 1406.

The famous Bayeux Tapestry depicts King Harold II praying at the church before he set sail for Normandy in 1064. *(taken from Chichester Harbour – A Reference Guide)*

Chichester Cathedral

The Cathedral has been a centre of Christian worship and community life for 900 years. It is the site of the Shrine of St Richard and houses a collection of art from Romanesque stone carvings to 20th century paintings, sculptures and tapestries. The building of the cathedral began around 1076 under the Bishop of Selsey and was dedicated in 1108 by Bishop Luffa. During the 15th century, the detached bell tower (the only one of its kind remaining in England) was added. It houses a peal of eight bells. The spire, which is a focal point of the countryside and can be seen from many parts of the harbour shoreline, was also added in this period. However, following years of neglect the spire collapsed in 1861 and the one we see today is a restoration by Sir George Gilbert Scott. It is the only cathedral in England that can be seen from the sea.

12	10km/6 miles	2.5 hours	Map Ref. SU 806 039 - Ordnance Survey Explorer 120

Walk 12

Across the Harbour

A one way walk across the top of the harbour channels giving fine views throughout. Ending in the vibrant village of Emsworth there are plenty of places for a welcome drink and a train or bus that will take you back to Bosham. Alternatively this walk can be done as a continuation of Walk 11 making it 17km.

Start Point
Bosham pay & display car park.

By Road
Turn south off the A259 towards Bosham. Follow the signs to the pay & display car park.

By Bus
Service 56 between Chichester and Bosham. This is an hourly service running Monday to Saturdays but not on bank holidays. Please check for up to date details. The bus stop is in the car park. The 700 Coastliner between Emsworth and Chichester stops on the A259 at the White Swan. Walk south down Delling Lane and then right into Bosham Lane. Start the walk at the Millstream Hotel.

By Rail
Bosham railway station is about a 20 minute walk from the start point. Walk south down Station Road, cross the A259 and continue as per the 700 Coastliner directions above. The Emsworth railway station is a 10 minute walk from the end point. Walk north from Emsworth Square, crossing the main road at the underpass and then walking up North Street to the station.

Refreshments
Lots of pubs, restaurants and cafés in Emsworth.
In Bosham there are two teashops and a pub.

Toilets
In Bosham car park and in Emsworth South Street car park.

Tides
The paths are non-tidal.

Walk Directions
From the car park walk to the road, Bosham Lane. Turn right. Just before the Millstream Hotel turn left into Moreton Road (1). On the corner of Windward Road take the footpath straight ahead between gardens. At the end of this path, continue ahead through the gap in the hedgerows and onto the gravel lane. Follow the footpath signs to reach the shoreline then bear right along the field edge. The path eventually reaches the top of the channel.

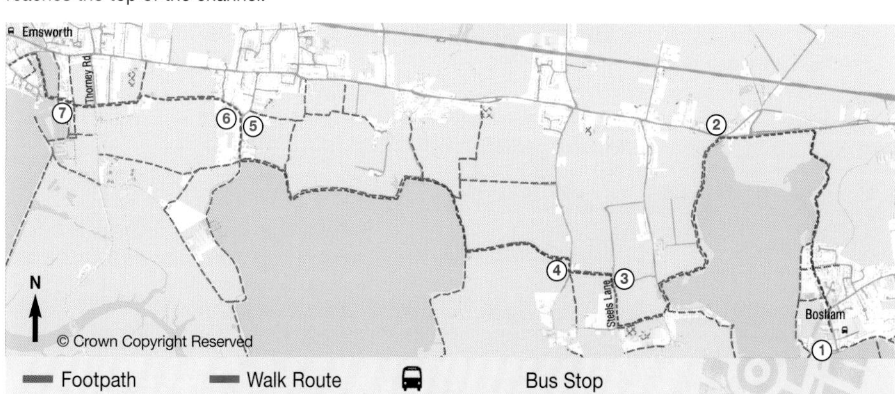

After a few minutes take the footpath to the right and walk up to the main road. Turn left. Take the first footpath to the left (2) to rejoin the shoreline (do not take the steps by Snowgoose).

The path continues around fields usually full of neat rows of vegetables. Go round onto the seawall path which then drops down onto the road.

Pass Harbour Way on your left and take the footpath on the right. This path crosses fields and passes large glasshouses, then goes down a gravel path to the road.

Turn right up Steels Lane and on the bend take the footpath straight ahead (3). Look out for the footpath on the left just before the 'Private Keep Out' sign. Follow the path across the fields. At the end of the field turn right to reach the road.

If you want a pub stop, at the road turn left for The Old House at Home or right for The Barleycorn.

To continue the walk, turn right at the road and then almost immediately take the footpath on the left by the row of Poplar trees (4). Follow the path across fields heading for the shoreline. Just before the shoreline, the path turns right and then shortly left to go up onto the seawall path. (Do not be tempted to shortcut across the muddy ditch.)

At the seawall path turn right and continue around the head of the channel until you come to an area with lots of benches. This is a good opportunity for a rest and to enjoy the view down the Thorney Channel.

Behind you is the Southbourne Sea Scouts building. Take the road to the right of it and walk up to the Square.

Turn left (5), on the bend of the road, take the footpath on the left (6), continue through the gate by the farmyard.

Keep following the footpath signs straight ahead over a number of footpath junctions. Cross straight over Thorney Road and continue on the path. When you reach the tarmac road follow it round to pick up the footpath (7) round the Slipper Mill Pond. (If the tide is very high then continue up Slipper Road to the main road. Turn left and then left again into Queen Street.)

Continue through the flats, then turn left into Queen Street. Follow the road into High Street to reach the village centre of Emsworth.

For the bus stop continue along High Street, bearing right. Go through the underpass and the bus stop is on the right. For the train station go through the underpass and continue up North Street.

Extra Items of Interest

Managing Chichester Harbour
Chichester Harbour was designated as an Area of Outstanding Natural Beauty (AONB) in 1964. In 1971 the Conservancy was set up by Act of Parliament to manage both the harbour and the AONB. This makes the Conservancy a unique organisation within the UK. The task of managing the harbour to satisfy the needs of all users can be a tough challenge.

The sheltered waters of the harbour make it ideal for racing and day sailing. Over 10,000 boats use the harbour each year and the 17 sailing clubs have over 11,000 members. Other popular activities are angling, birdwatching, walking, wildfowling, painting and photography.

Chichester Harbour is nationally and internationally designated to recognise its importance for nature conservation. It is particularly significant for wintering wildfowl and waders, of which five species reach numbers which are internationally important. Farming, fishing, marine businesses and tourism are the main businesses within the AONB.

The Conservancy strives to maintain a balance between the various interest groups so that everyone, including wildlife can continue to enjoy the Area of Outstanding Natural Beauty.

Birds of Chichester Harbour
Thousands of birds flock to Chichester Harbour each year. They come here because of the abundant source of food in the mudflats, saltmarsh and surrounding farmland. Around the harbour there is little pollution or disturbance making it an ideal site for birdlife.

Photo by Ludi Lochner

Whatever time of year you are out you are sure to spot some birds. At low tide waders such as Curlew and Redshanks will be searching through the mud with their long beaks. Brent Geese and Wigeon eat plants such as Eelgrass that can be found growing in the mud. Fish-eating birds such as Terns and Cormorants will dive into the water for food whilst Herons and Little Egrets stand and fish in the shallows.

As the tide comes in and covers the mud, the birds take the opportunity to go elsewhere to rest and preen. Waders fly to nearby fields or onto area of high shingle. Ducks and Geese rest on the water surface or ashore.

Short Walks 13 - 19

Short Strolls and Wheelchair Walks

Around the harbour there are some hard-surfaced paths suitable for wheelchairs and pushchairs. These all lead to viewpoints over the water and most have parking for blue badge holders nearby. The paths are of course open to all and these selected short walks will be enjoyed by everyone. Many include ideas for picnic stops. Please note that some of the paths only have parking for blue badge holders near the start. Times have not been given for these walks and distances are approximate depending how much of the route you choose to follow.

1.5km/1 mile **Map Ref. SU 798 012** (car park) - Ordnance Survey Explorer 120 **13**

Itchenor Viewpoint

By Road

From the A27 take the A286 south of Chichester towards the Witterings. After about 5 miles, at the small roundabout, continue straight on towards West Wittering. After ½ mile take the right hand turn signposted Itchenor. Follow this road for about 2 miles until you see a sign on the left to a pay and display car park.

Blue Badge Holders - At the far right hand corner of the car park there are some designated disabled parking spaces.

Walk Details

From the far, right hand corner of the car park go through the gate and along the surfaced footpath. When you get to the shoreline, turn left and continue. At the end of the surfaced section bear right and you will come to a small, open grassy area. There is a bench here to rest and admire the view across to Cobnor.

Either picnic on the grassy area, or if the tide is low on the shingle.

14 **0.5km/0.3 mile** **Map Ref. SU 766 051** - Ordnance Survey Explorer 120

Prinsted Stroll

By Road

From the A259 turn south onto Prinsted Lane. At the end of the road there is parking for a few cars by the Sea Scouts hut.

Walk Details

From the parking area go up onto the shoreline path. Here there are benches with views over the bay which make a good picnic spot. Turn left onto the hard surfaced section which is suitable for wheelchairs. This is quite a short section with a turning area for wheelchairs at the end.

To extend the walk, continue along this path retracing your steps when you are ready.

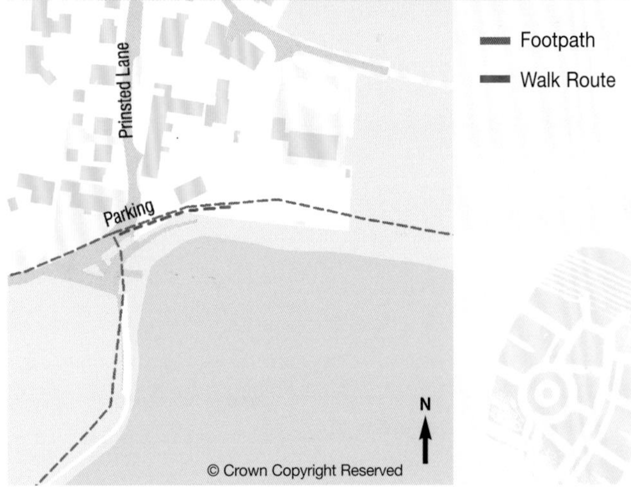

1km/0.6 mile **Map Ref. SU 728 038** - Ordnance Survey Explorer 120 **15**

North Common Explorer

By Road

From the A27 turn off towards Hayling Island. Once over the bridge and just before the petrol station take the first left. Follow the road round, past the Langstone Hotel. Look for the small parking area on the left after the Northney village sign. Note there is a 2m height barrier at the entrance.

Walk Details

From the car park go through the box gate, (if you have a RADAR key you can open the padlock on the metal gate). From the the path there are great views over to Langstone and Emsworth with the South Downs in the distance. The wheelchair path stops after 600m and then reverts to a footpath.

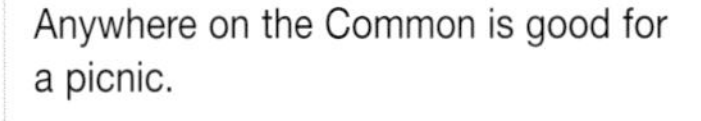

Anywhere on the Common is good for a picnic.

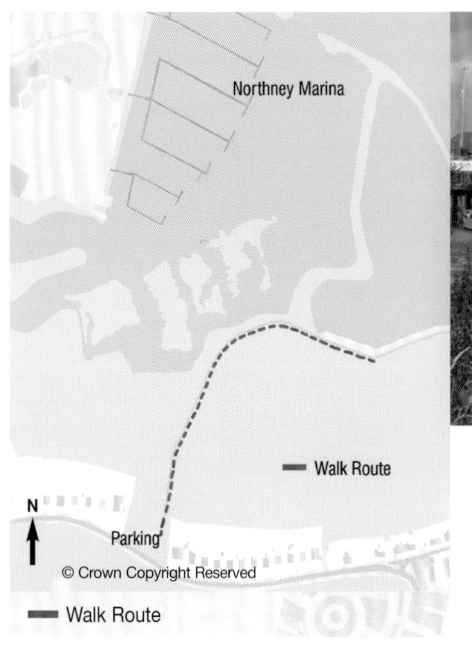

16 **2km/1.5 miles** **Map Ref. SU 793 025** - Ordnance Survey Explorer 120

Cobnor Wheelchair Path

For Blue Badge Holders Only

By Road

From the A259 turn south down Chidham Lane, pass the Amenity car park then turn left down the private road following the sign for Cobnor Farm. Go past the Activity Centre on your left and take the next left. There is a small parking area for blue badge holders only. Otherwise see Walk 10 for parking and walk directions.

Walk Details

From the parking area take the path which starts near the toilets (RADAR key only). Follow it south. The path crosses a dinghy park, then turns left towards the harbour. Shortly after the plaque commemorating the opening of the path, turn right along the seawall. Continue along this 800m of surfaced path with some of the finest views of the harbour. At the end of the path there is a bench and turning area.

For picnicking, walk down the steps to sit on the shore.

1km/0.6 mile **Map Ref. SU 806 039** - Ordnance Survey Explorer 120 **17**

Bosham Explorer

By Road

From the A259 follow the signs to Bosham and then to the pay & display car park. Parking is free for blue badge holders.

Walk Details

From the car park exit, cross the road and take the path through the wrought iron gate to the Parish Church (1). The gates are alongside the Craft Centre (note only guide dogs are allowed in the church grounds). Visit the Church by the north door for wheelchair access or continue by the left hand path for the main entrance.

Continue past the main entrance to exit the churchyard. Turn left and then right over a small bridge (2). You are now opposite Quay Meadow, a favourite picnic area. Visit the historic Quay, then take the shoreline road past the Anchor Bleu. Turn left at Bosham Lane to return to the car park.

If the tide is high the shore road may be flooded. If so, head back towards the Church and take the road alongside it. You will pass the Anchor Bleu from behind. At the end of the road, turn left to return to the car park.

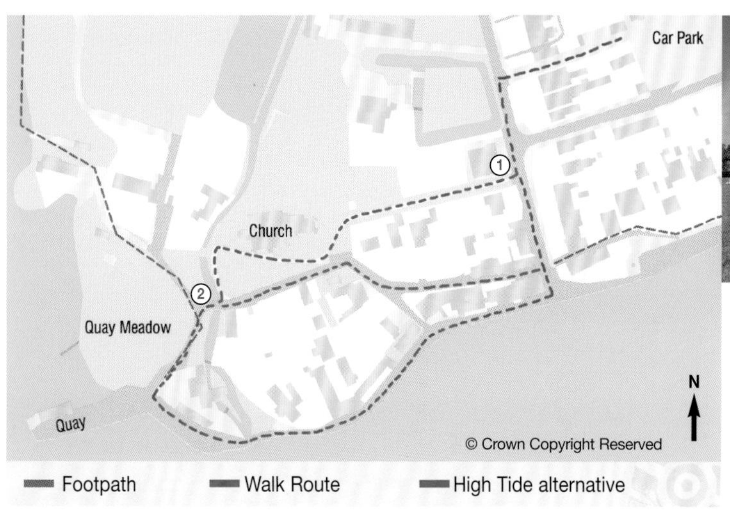

18 **2.5km/1.5 miles** **Map Ref. SZ 773 979** - Ordnance Survey Explorer 120

East Head Circuit

By Road

From the A286 follow signs to West Wittering Beach car park. Park at the far end of the car park. There is a charge for parking, which is reduced for blue badge holders.

Walk Details

From the car park, pass the large wooden gate onto East Head. Walk either clockwise or anti-clockwise around the dunes. Please note that the route is mainly soft sand and is only suitable for all-terrain wheelchairs. The sands are tidal. If it is high tide you can walk through the dunes instead.

An all-terrain wheelchair is available to hire from the West Wittering Estate Office. Call 01243 514143.

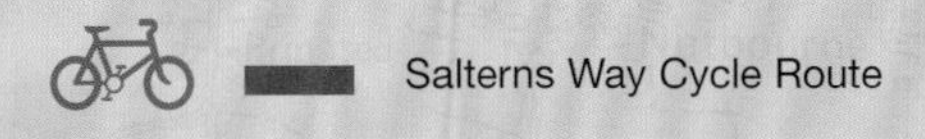

Please note

Sections of the path are also used by walkers and wheelchairs.
Please show respect for all users. Users of the Salterns Way do so at their own risk.
Chichester Harbour Conservancy do not accept any responsibility for any loss, damage or injury, howsoever caused, arising directly or indirectly from use of the Salterns Way cycle route.

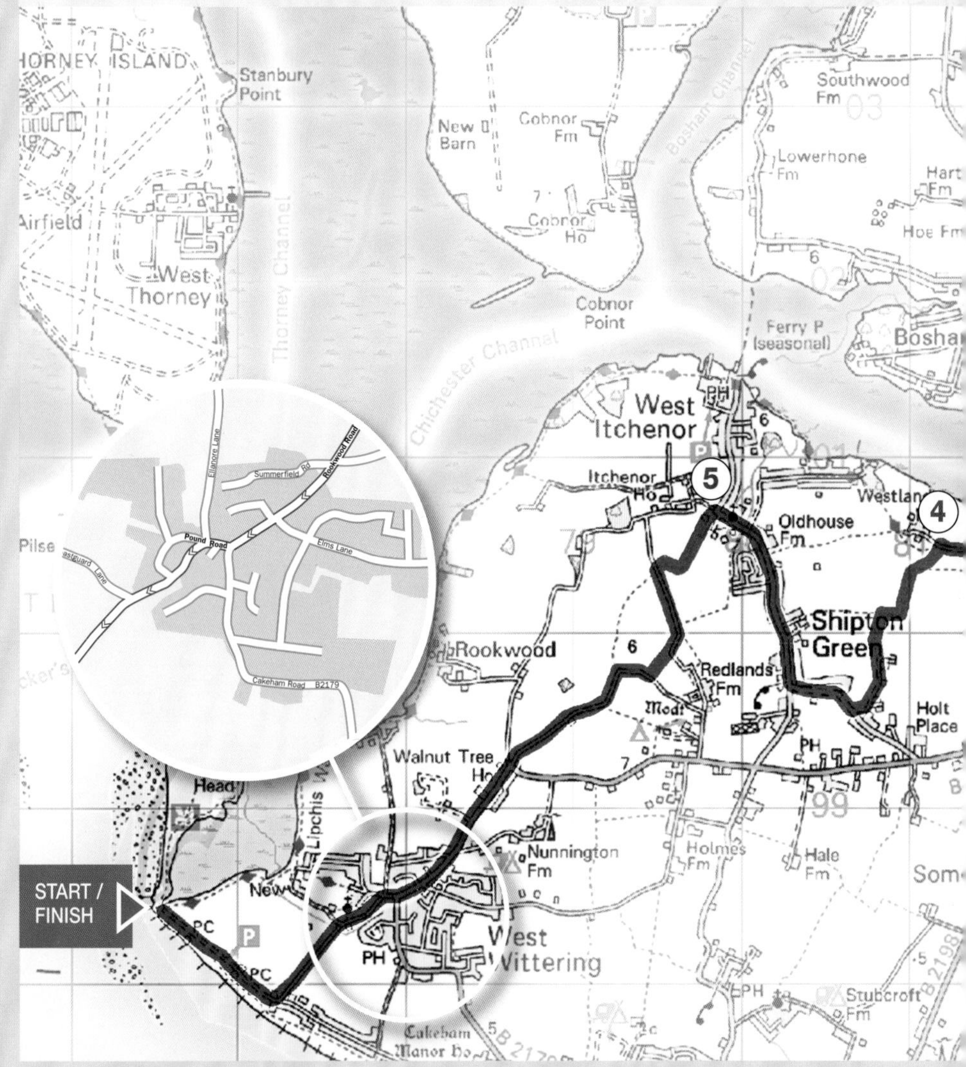

1 | 18km/11 miles (one way) | 2 hours | Map Ref. SU 858 048 - Ordnance Survey Explorer 120

Cycle Ride 1

Salterns Way Cycle Route

Pack a picnic and enjoy this virtually flat ride to the sandy beach at West Wittering. Starting at the heart of Chichester, much of the route is off road using cycle paths that cross fields and countryside. The route is well-signposted so once you start you shouldn't have to stop too often to consult the directions.

Photo by Matt Simmons

1.8km/1 mile **Map Ref. SU 836 011** - Ordnance Survey Explorer 120 **19**

Chichester Marina Circular

By Road

From the A286 turn off at Chichester Marina. Park in the free visitors car park.

Walk Details

The walk around the Marina is circular, so you can go either way. If the lock gates are open, wait patiently and the lock keeper will close them for you to cross. The crossing is wide enough for most wheelchairs. If walking anti-clockwise from the car park you will very shortly come to a bird hide looking over a reedbed.

Just past the lock gates there is a café.

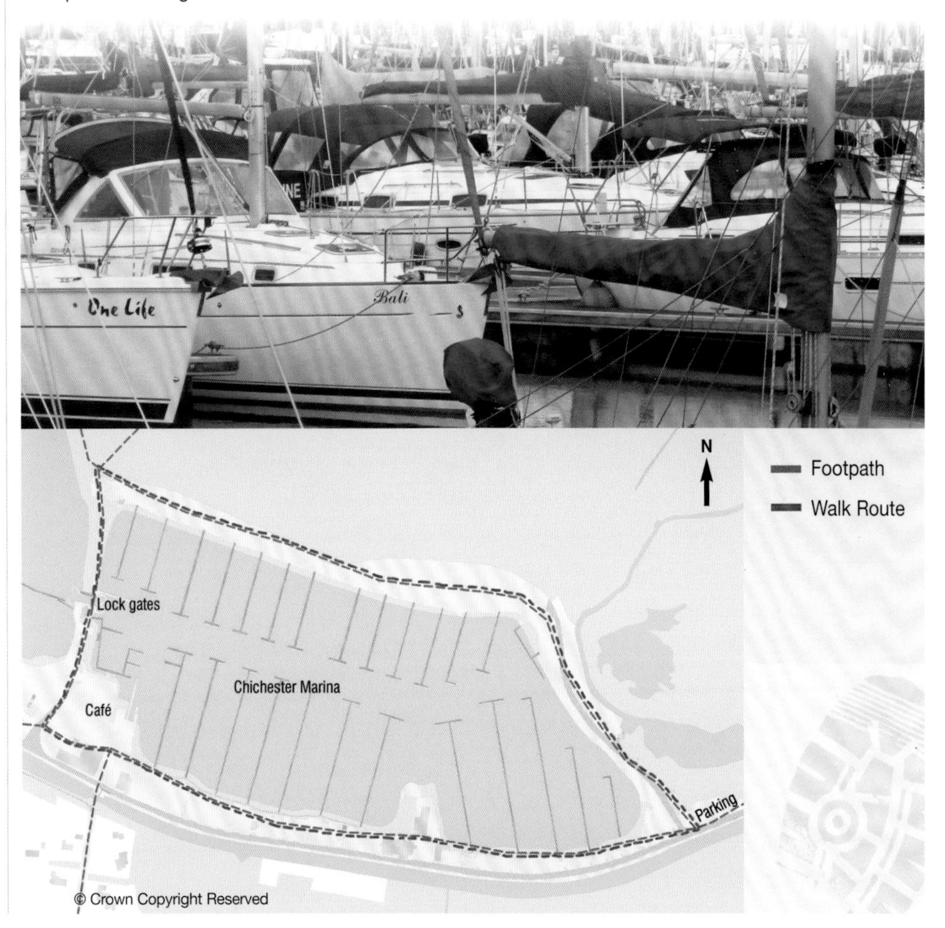

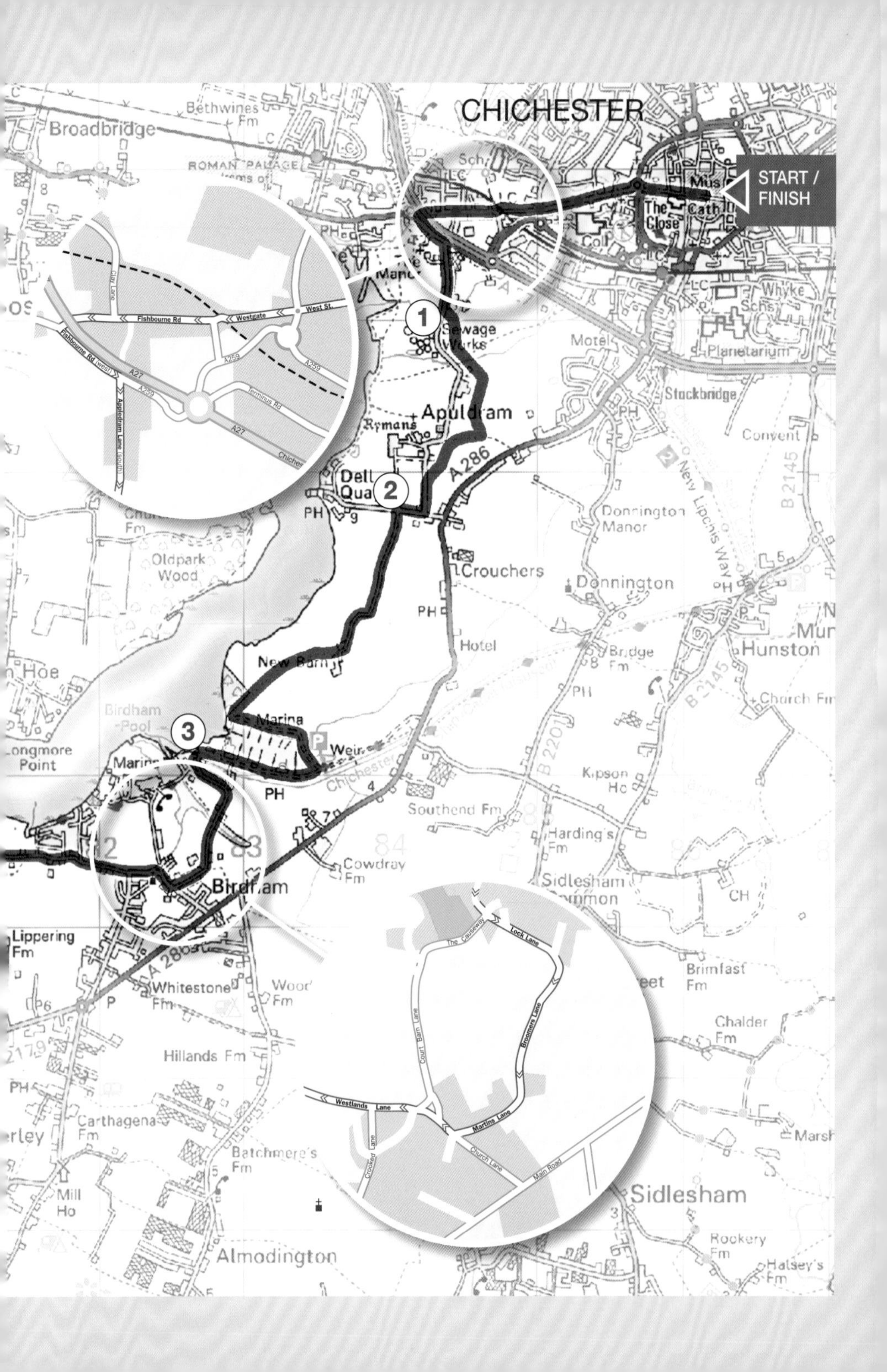

CHICHESTER
START / FINISH
1
2
3
Broadbridge
Bethwines Fm
ROMAN PALACE
Apuldram
Dell Quay
Sewage Works
Stockbridge
A 286
Donnington Manor
Donnington
Crouchers
New Barn
Marina
Birdham Pool
Longmore Point
Hunston
Birdham
Sidlesham
Sidlesham Common
Almodington
Southend Fm
Cowdray Fm
Whitestone Fm
Hillands Fm
Carthagena Fm
Batchmere's Fm
Lippering Fm
Oldpark Wood
Fishbourne Rd
Westgate
West St.
A259
A27
Terminus Rd
Appledram Lane (south)
Clay Lane
The Causeway
Lock Lane
Broomers Lane
Court Barn Lane
Westlands Lane
Martins Lane
Church Lane
Main Road
Crooked Lane

Start Point
The Cross, Chichester, PO19 1HW.
If you are coming by car other start points with parking are Westgate PO19 3HR, Chichester Marina PO20 7EJ or at West Wittering Beach car park PO20 8AJ.

By Road
There are a number of car parks in Chichester.

By Rail
From Chichester station cycle north towards The Cross.

Refreshments
Lots of pubs, restaurants and cafés in Chichester. Along the route there is a café at the Apuldram Centre, The Crown and Anchor at Dell Quay, cafés at Chichester Marina, The Ship at Itchenor, a number of pubs and cafés at West Wittering and a café in West Wittering car park.

Toilets
In Tower Street, Chichester opposite the Cathedral, at Chichester Marina and at West Wittering car park.

Ride Directions
From The Cross cycle along West Street passing the Cathedral on your left. Go straight across at the roundabout and into Westgate, then across another small roundabout. At the end of Westgate bear right and take the bridge over the railway line. Continue ahead and through the underpass. Turn left for a short way then cross this busy road at the crossing point. Continue along the cycle path turning right into Appledram Lane South.

After about 400m leave the road and go through the kissing gate on your left (1). You now continue along an off road section of the path with fields to your left. If you want a break call in at the Apuldram Centre, there is a gate off the path into the centre which has a small café.

The path rejoins Appledram Lane South through a kissing gate, continue to the T-junction then turn right. If you want a pub stop continue along this road to The Crown and Anchor.

Otherwise after a short way turn left onto a wide farm track (2). This path passes through Apuldram Manor Farm. Across the fields are views towards Chichester Harbour. As you pass the cow shed the path bears to the right and narrows. At the end of the field you continue along the edge of Salterns Copse.

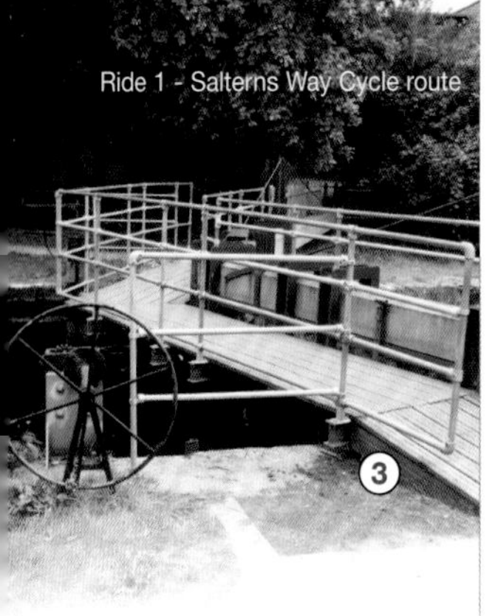

At the end of the Copse turn left and you are at Chichester Marina. Turn left and cycle around the marina. After the car park barrier, turn right and continue alongside the Chichester Canal with its array of houseboats. Watch out for swans and ducks on this section!

Continue to the end and alongside Chichester Yacht Club. Here you need to dismount to cross the canal bridge (3). This section is a public footpath so you will need to walk for the next couple of minutes. Once past the tall fence, turn right and then walk to the road.

Turn left onto Lock Lane and continue along this quiet lane which changes its name to Broomers Lane and Martins Lane. At the junction with Church Lane, turn right, passing the church on your left and the old village pump on your right. Church Lane leads onto a concrete road, Westlands Lane. Before you get to the farm you will see two gates to your left (4). Take the kissing gate and follow the route as it winds around field edges finally coming out by Itchenor Caravan Park.

Follow the route around an open field and through a wooden gate. Turn right onto Itchenor Road and follow the road round to the right. As you pass the village church, look out for a left turn. Don't go ahead to the farm but through the wooden gate alongside the village hall (5). (If you continue straight ahead past the church you will come to the harbour and The Ship).

Continue along this off road section which crosses a field. When you get to the junction with a concrete farm road, turn left. Continue along and look carefully for the signposted path on the right. Take this path across a field, the gate at the other end takes you onto Sheepwash Lane. Turn right onto this pretty, shaded lane. Continue ahead until you reach Rookwood Road.

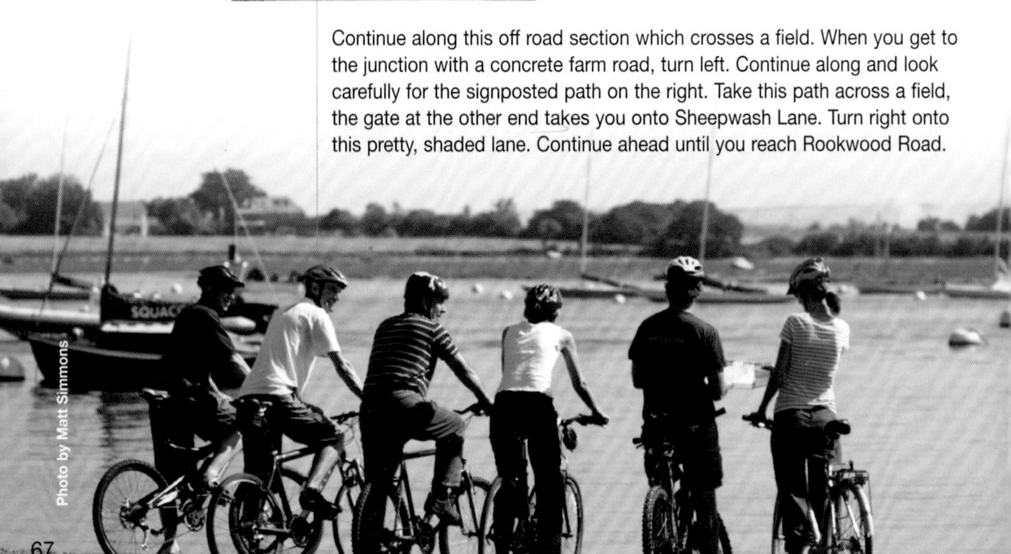

Photo by Matt Simmons

Take care on this junction as you turn right onto Rookwood Road. This section can be busy with traffic especially on sunny days with people going to the beach. You will pass a small row of shops and a café. After a short way turn right into Pound Lane which is signposted for West Wittering Beach. On the left are public toilets and on the right a small café.

Bear left past the toilets and follow the road right down to the car park entrance. You can access the beach at various points from the car park or for the sand dunes of East Head, cycle to the far end of the car park and then through a gate.

More information

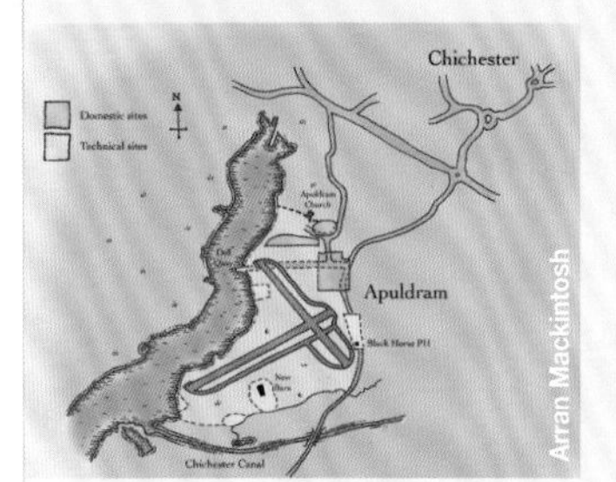

Apuldram Airfield

When cycling along the farm track at Apuldram Manor Farm look to the fields on your right and try to imagine an RAF camp and planes taking off and landing. That was the scene in 1943. Two runways were laid with a metal track which allowed the grass to grow between the steel mesh. This was important as the farmers were allowed to graze their animals on the airfield when it was not in use.

The main domestic site was located adjacent to the sharp bend in Appledram Lane. Some buildings were erected, but in the main tented accommodation was provided for pilots and ground crew. Nearby cottages were also requisitioned and field kitchens set up. The building of the second runway across the Dell Quay road required the road to be sealed off and a house to be demolished.

On 2 June 1943, three squadrons of Hawker Typhoons arrived, they stayed for a month. Then on 1 April 1944, three Czech squadrons arrived with their clipped-wing Spitfire LF Mk IXB aircraft and Apuldram. Bombs for the aircraft arrived by road and were stored in a bomb dump near the Black Horse.

On 5 June, the pilots were briefed at 2030 hours on their role for D-Day. Early the following day, the Czech squadrons were placed on 30 minutes notice, their allotted task being to cover the British and Canadian landing forces on the Eastern sector of the beaches. Throughout the day they flew 50 minute patrols and it is claimed that Apuldram's Czech squadrons carried out more operational sorties on 6 June than any other unit.

Appledram or Apuldram

Old records show many different spellings - Apulderham, Apeldreham (1121), Appeltrieham (1198), Appuldram (1440) - but for several centuries the spelling used by the church and the parishioners has been Apuldram. Civic authorities use both 'Appledram' and 'Apuldram' in their records.

W D Peckham is quoted as writing 'the deep loam with a clay or brick-earth subsoil is admirable apple growing land to this day'. However, evidence of when or where in the parish apple farming took place has not come to light - records show grain and, later, wool as the main products of the area. Richard Ratcliffe's history of the parish examines, but does not favour, a suggestion that the name is derived from polder a Dutch word meaning low lying land protected or reclaimed from the sea, although this would indeed be an apt description of a large part of the parish. *Taken from Wikipedia (2013)*

2 | **21km/13 miles** | **3-4 hours** | **Map Ref. SU 836 011** - Ordnance Survey Explorer 120

Cycle Ride 2

Chichester Harbour Circular

This circular bike ride is virtually flat. Use it as the basis for a great day out for cyclists of all ages. Take time to stop and explore the ancient village of Bosham and enjoy the harbour views. With a ferry ride and lots of pub or café stops this will be a pleasant ride to remember.

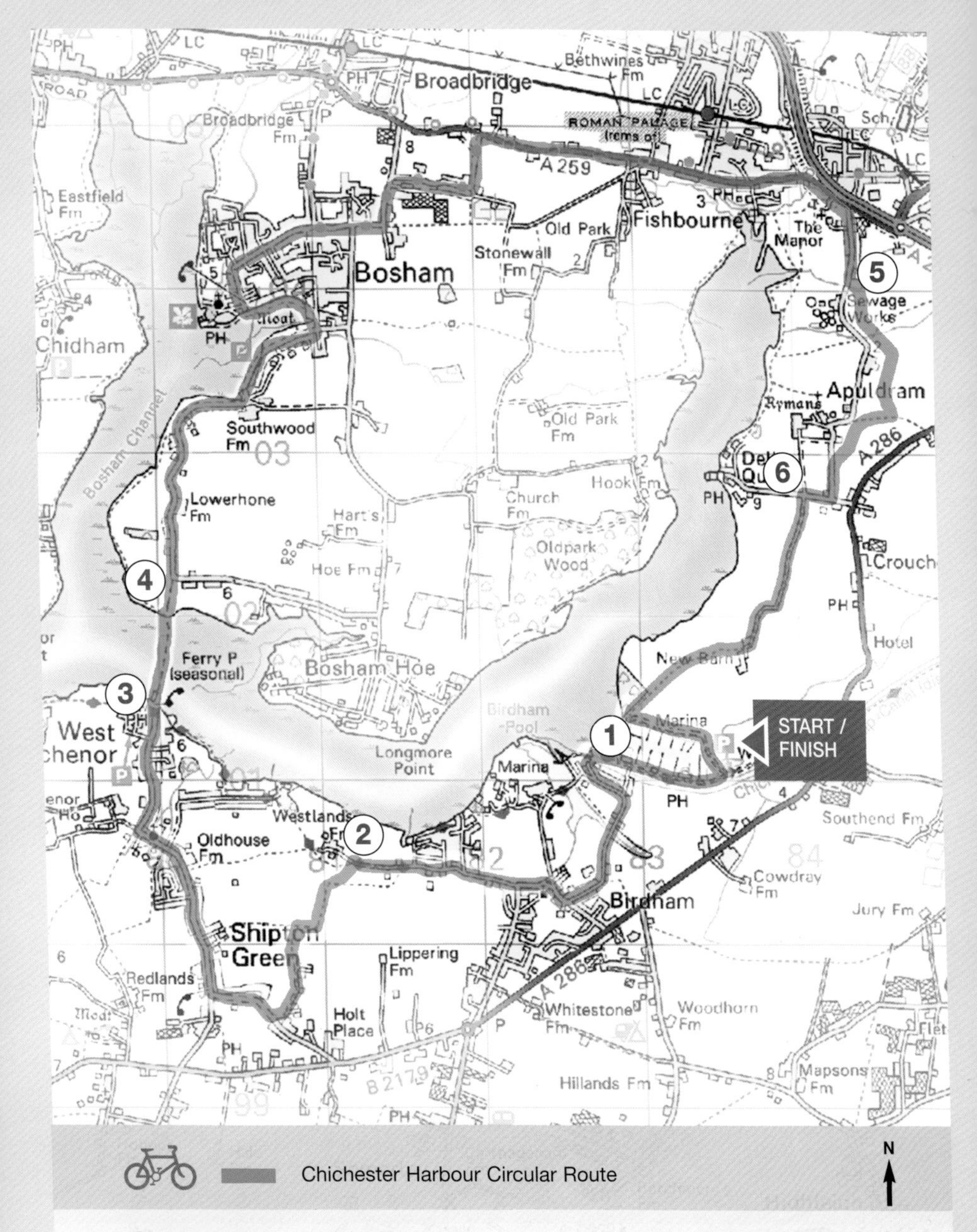

Please note

The ferry runs seasonally. Call 07970 378350 or see www.itchenorferry.co.uk for running times. Sections of the path are also used by walkers and wheelchairs.

Please show respect for all users. Users of the Chichester Circular Route do so at their own risk. Chichester Harbour Conservancy do not accept any responsibility for any loss, damage or injury, howsoever caused, arising directly or indirectly from use of the cycle route.

Photo by Juliet Walker

Start Point
Visitors car park at Chichester Marina, PO20 7EJ.

By Road
Free parking in the designated car park at the marina.

By Rail
From Chichester station cycle north towards The Cross.

Refreshments
There are a number of options on this route at Itchenor, Bosham, Fishbourne, Dell Quay and Chichester Marina.

Toilets
Itchenor by the Harbour Office, Bosham in the public car park (off Bosham Lane), Chichester Marina.

Please note
This ride is seasonal and tidal. The ferry operates from April to the end of October. Please check running times before setting out at www.itchenorferry.co.uk or call 07970 378350.

The section between the ferry and Bosham floods when the tide is 4.7m or higher. Avoid this section 2 hours either side of high tide. If you do arrive at high tide, from the ferry turn right along Smugglers Lane, left into Hoe Lane and then right onto Old Park Lane. This will eventually come to the A259. Turn right to rejoin our route. Note this route does not take in the old village of Bosham.

Ride Directions

From the visitors car park, cycle down the marina road with the Chichester Canal on your left. Watch out for swans and ducks on this section!

Continue to the end and alongside Chichester Yacht Club. Here you need to dismount to cross the canal bridge (1). This section is a public footpath so you will need to walk for the next couple of minutes. Once past the tall fence, turn right and then walk to the road.

Turn left onto Lock Lane and continue along this quiet lane which changes its name to Broomers Lane and Martins Lane. At the junction with Church Lane, turn right, passing the church on your left and the old village pump on your right. Church Lane leads onto a concrete road, Westlands Lane.

Before you get to the farm you will see two gates to your left (2). Take the kissing gate and follow the route as it winds around field edges finally coming out by Itchenor Caravan Park.

Follow the route around an open field and through a wooden gate. Turn right onto Itchenor Road and follow the road round to the right. Continue past the village pond and church down to the harbour.

Turn left by the Harbour Office and to the right of Jetty House you will see the public jetty (3). Dismount and walk to the end of the jetty, the ferry will be on the end of the left. You may need to wait up to 15 minutes if the ferry is dropping mariners at their boat further up the reach.

Once across the channel, walk along the gravel path ahead of you (4). At the end turn left onto Lower Hone Lane, follow this scenic lane as it becomes Shore Road. From here you will see the village of Bosham and up to the South Downs. To the left is Chidham. Keep cycling around the head of the channel keeping the water on your left. If the tide is low enough you may be able to take the old wadeway across the top of the channel. Otherwise pass in front of the Old School House and round to the village.

Take time to explore the Quay, church and craft centre. When you are ready to continue cycle up Bosham Lane bearing right at the Millstream Hotel. Continue along this road passing a pub on your left and then the village school. This is now part of National Cycle Route 2. Continue around a left bend and shortly you will see a right turn into Chequer Lane.

Take this lane which leads past some houses and open fields until joining the A259. Turn right and use the cycle lane that runs along most of this busy section. You will pass through Fishbourne and past a number of pubs.

Turn right at Appledram Lane South. After about 400m leave the road and go through the kissing gate on your left (5). You now continue along an off road section of the path with fields to your left.

The path rejoins Appledram Lane South through a kissing gate, continue to the T-junction then turn right. If you want a pub stop continue along this road to The Crown and Anchor. Otherwise after a short way turn left onto a wide farm track (6).

This path passes through Apuldram Manor Farm. Across the fields are views towards Chichester Harbour. As you pass the cow shed the path bears to the right and narrows. At the end of the field you continue along the edge of Salterns Copse.

At the end of the Copse turn left and you are at Chichester Marina. Turn left and cycle around the marina and back to your start point.